Vichy Boyhood

An Inside View of the Pétain Regime

PASCAL JARDIN

EPILOGUE BY EMMANUEL BERL

Translated by Jean Stewart

FABER AND FABER
3 Queen Square
London

*First published in 1975
by Faber and Faber Limited
3 Queen Square London WC1N 3AU
Printed in Great Britain by
Latimer Trend & Company Ltd Plymouth*

ISBN 0 571 10739 7

*Originally published by Bernard Grasset, Paris,
as 'La Guerre à Neuf Ans: Une histoire
de Vichy par un Saint-Simon
en culottes courtes'*

*Three short extracts from Pascal Jardin's
'Guerre après Guerre' (Bernard Grasset,
1973) have been included in the English
edition by kind permission of the publishers*

To Pierre Caro

On est de son enfance comme on est d'un pays
Saint-Exupéry

Author's Note

I haven't told all. That would be overdoing it

English Publisher's Acknowledgement

We are grateful to Edward Mortimer for the advice
and assistance he has given us in preparing the
English edition

SEPTEMBER 1969. I am thirty-five years old. I write film scripts. I had escaped from Paris for a few hours to visit a tiny business in Evreux of which I'm part owner, the Dulac et Jardin Press. Dulac is the name of my cousin, my friend, my partner. Our trade name was my invention. It reminds one of *Bouvard et Pécuchet*, Laurel and Hardy, Flers and Caillavet; it suggests harmony, shared responsibility, some old-established provincial firm—in short, it sounds solid and reliable.

My new Alfa-Romeo gobbled up the miles. As I drove into the town I saw on my right a deserted house. It used to be the brothel for the American base at Evreux.

Over ten years ago I knew a magnificent Breton girl there, Nana. She wanted to make me eat her excrement, no less; not out of depravity, she was far beyond that, and the wonderful thing was that she didn't know it. I think she'd fallen for me and wanted to teach me not to be afraid of anything. For her, making love without taking risks was like making war without killing.

In periods of doubt, at times when things fall apart, sex with no holds barred, the indiscriminate mingling of mouths and genitals and backsides means sharing defilement, being bound fast to one another and yet keeping far enough apart to see each other clearly. With that sort of eroticism, norms are abolished and time stands still.

The town of Evreux, aggressive as ever, hit me in the face.

Childhood is the first of one's many lives. Happy or unhappy, you can never get over it. Childhood is the springhead. You always go back to it. And I always go back to Evreux.

When I got to the printing-house I was told that my grand-mother, eighty-four years old, was dying in hospital.

Under a drizzling sky I went through a mid-nineteenth century hospital building that was like a jail. Beyond that monstrosity I found an ultra-modern building. Four floors. A tiled passage like a metro corridor, a door. I paused and then went in. In a bed above which a drip-feed apparatus hung from a bracket, a grey-haired woman lay tossing restlessly, her face half-paralysed.

I used to know her very well. Now I hardly knew her. Every one of her jerky words expressed despair. She wanted to see her son, my father, who lived in Switzerland. She'd been there five days, fighting against death.

'You see, darling, I've got to see him before . . .'

And then she sank into a doped sleep. I went to the window. The pane reflected a blurred image of me. For a quarter of a century or more, now, I've been staggering along alone, some-times like a dumb animal, sometimes like a man, falling down and picking myself up again. Life has battered me and yet I don't feel in the least bit damaged.

How have the things that happened here from 1939 onwards helped to make me into what I am, a voluminous script writer—over eighty films in less than ten years—enjoying a sort of com-mercial notoriety, with a Parisian shell that has enabled me to keep on my feet in tough times?

The right side of my grandmother's mouth drooped and a dribble of death ran slowly down her cheek. Outside, it had begun to rain properly.

Why did I marry twice? My first marriage was a total failure from which nothing has survived except two enchanting chil-dren. The second? Yes, the second was something important; it goes a long way back. I met my second wife about 1940 in Paris. We were living practically in the same street. She was five years old. I thought she was a horrid ugly thing. Was that an omen? Does everything have to be recut and turned inside

14

out so as to fit better afterwards? My second marriage has been peace in the midst of war. I can never weary of it.

I loved her ever since the day when I married my first wife. What a mess. And yet the more mistakes I made the more clearly I saw where I wanted to get to. Then one day I knew that I was going to remarry. Nobody else knew. That didn't bother me. Having my eyes fixed on my goal I felt that I could overcome all obstacles on the way. So I remarried, against everyone's wishes, against the wishes of my friends, of my friends' friends, of my entire family, of my mistress and of her husband whom I loved, and who loved me, of my first wife, of her lover, of my first and second mothers-in-law, and the husband of the girl I was going to marry. He had just come home from a long, horrible spell of war service in Algeria. He was a sick man, he adored his wife, he could not contemplate divorcing her. I made him divorce her all the same. I expect I half killed him. I expect, too, that I destroyed something essential in the two children I had by my first marriage. Everyone thought I was a bastard, and so I was. That didn't matter. I had to stay alive, by fair means or foul. I didn't see it as a moral problem, but as an absolute necessity. Nothing else mattered. And I meant that not in a casual careless way, but in the same way that I live and breathe, that the North wind blows, that the tide rises like a galloping horse in Mont-Saint-Michel bay. Nothing else matters!

Finally, in order to attain my end I had to associate with the men in her circle. There were swarms of them, buzzing round her magnetic feminine personality. I had to ally myself with some of them in order to eliminate others. I made her meet 'my' men, who fell in love with her on my behalf and under my partial control. I betrayed everybody except myself. The hardest part was convincing the loved one herself. She did not love me, and persisted in seeing me merely as an intermittent partner. Neither pressure nor rebuffs, nor public humiliation, nor shame, nor having to share, nor threats nor blows ever made me change my mind for a single hour. She has remained my sole certainty, and I have never let go of her. Her multi-racial face, that look she

15

has of coming from everywhere and belonging to nowhere in particular is, for me, a kind of supra-nationality which abolishes racism and yet glorifies races. I can see her as black, as Jewish, as an Arab or an Asiatic. Her eyes are crucibles in whose depths the alchemist's lead turns to gold. There exists in my mind an obscure connection between that unquestionably beautiful woman who is my wife and this town of Evreux. And perhaps this is why when I go to the ends of the earth, to Asia, to Pnom Penh, I think of Evreux. I think of it frantically, because thinking of Evreux means thinking of her. I know this association is illogical because my wife hates the town and refuses to stop there when we drive through. And I know, too, that I lived in Evreux with my first wife and that we tried desperately to love one another there. I know I'm thinking of the wrong woman when I associate the face of my present wife with that town. My memory is a mass of forgetfulness. I know it's dishonest, dishonest but sincere. And always, and continually, the invisible skein of emotional bonds that guides my life willy-nilly pulls me to right or left, making me confuse everything the better to rediscover everything. I know nothing of chronology or reason. My heart is not a tool intended for a definite purpose, but rather a saw that can be used either to cut up wood or to make music. And just as everything, or the slightest thing, makes me think of my wife, she, my wife, makes me think of Alain Delon. These two people who have nothing in common are alike. They are alike under the skin, in the fibre of their being, in their contained fury, in their reticence and their beauty. I knew Alain twelve years ago. He was learning to be an actor and he crashed my car the day after we met. He was already stamped with the imprint of immoderateness, he had already gone beyond all norms. And he fascinated me. He is the only man who has ever dominated me with a look, sometimes making me wish I were a woman so as to know him better. He combines physical magnetism with the cunning of a seasoned adventurer. He is a barefoot beggar from Bourg-la-Reine and yet a king; made of the stuff of the great captains of old, the men who under Richelieu would have been

16

sent to the gallows or ennobled on the spot. The richness of his personality comes from the fact that he is manifold and that his various selves are at odds with one another. Hence fierce sudden changes, unpredictable transitions from rage to tenderness. When he married Nathalie I was staggered by their likeness to one another. He had found another Alain, himself in female shape. She was his love and his sister. Their twin radiance smacked of incest, just as war reeks of gunpowder. More than anyone I know, in these dreary times, Alain Delon brings in his wake tumult and drama; a Shakespearean hero strayed into a period of crime fiction, he looks out at the world with a steely gaze in which we catch the glint of childish tears.

◆

Thanks to the war, I was launched into life very young. So young indeed that by about 1941 I must have seemed more like an elderly baby than a small boy.

Born on 14th May 1934, I was only five years old when I listened in 1939 to Jean Giraudoux's address to the schoolboys of France. I was six at the time of the Mers-el-Kebir tragedy, nine when the battle of Stalingrad was fought and at least fifty by the time I was eleven, at the end of the war.

Fortunately, I've been growing younger ever since.

◆

Evreux, August 1939. It was splendid summer weather. With my elder brother Simon and my mother, I was spending the holidays as usual with my maternal grandparents, the Duchesnes. My grandfather was a fashionable provincial surgeon. My grandmother was a rich spoilt child, an orphan, whom my grandfather had married almost without knowing her for the sake of her considerable dowry. Shortly after his marriage Grandfather decided to sell the many farms that belonged to his wife. He was hopeless at using the multiplication table and was afraid of appearing ridiculous when talking to his farm bailiffs. When he had sold off more than 200 hectares of the richest land in France, he invested all the proceeds in Russian stocks so as to be free from worry. He achieved that aim very fast. When he had ruined himself, he no longer had to worry about his capital.

He was a handsome elegant man with a moustache. She was short and squat, musical, with a bad heart and a bad temper. I called them respectively Monsieur Père and Madame Mère. Their tall white house, built in the eighteen-twenties, looked over the eighteenth-century buildings of the Préfecture on one side, and on the other over a terrace, then a garden, then a kitchen garden that led on to a hen-run, which itself opened on to an ancient wash-house jutting out above a trout stream, the Iton.

I adored Madame Mère, and she loved me just as madly. Our mutual passion lasted until her death in 1957. Although my whole childhood was spent in a state of total ignorance, she always maintained an unquestioning faith in me. To her, I was one of the elect; some day I was going to be famous. To me, she was the person who accepted me without reservation, who would allow me to wreak havoc in her house, keep rabbits in my bed or shoot the Prefect with a popgun. Later she was to love my girls, my friends, my sorrows, the lot. Completely unintellectual, swearing like a trooper, superstitious, psychic, jealous, irascible, given to hitting the maids with her stick and abusing passers-by through the window, she was a tremendous character, a crazy affectionate dragon, wonder-struck at the least thing, passing in surges from tears to shrieks to laughter and ending up with bouts of extravagant enthusiasm that rose up from her guts and left her gasping for breath. She was a real marvel, that woman.

Those 1939 holidays were like any others. Madame Mère lived on the first floor, since her diseased heart debarred her from too much stair-climbing. Her headquarters had been set up in the dining-room in front of an outsize wireless set. This room was a sort of lawcourt where sessions were held only at meal-times. The furniture was made of wild cherry-wood, richly carved. The backs of the chairs were bunches of grapes. The top of the

sideboard was a pyramid of pears. The mantelpiece, supported
by two Herculean figures harnessed like mules, was crowned
with wedding-cake ornaments. The tapestry curtains, as thick as
carpets, were patterned with haunted forests. The Venetian glass
chandelier had a network of hollow tubes full of dead flies.

Twice a day this grotesque place became an assize court. Here,
at lunch and at dinner, Madame Mère would prosecute her
husband.

'Robert, you're nothing but a crackpot!'

Monsieur Père never answered back at the beginning of a
meal. He just looked at his wife with the air of a man who has
decided once and for all that you cannot stop the tide from rising.
The two maids waiting at table passed the dishes adroitly while
Madame Mère growled and thundered. Sometimes, towards the
end of the meal, a piece of cheese would be sent flying at Monsieur Père's head. But after thirty years of married life he had
learnt to dodge it. I have seen few Camemberts really score a
bull's eye.

When I asked my mother what she thought about these battles
she would lift her great dreamy eyes from the Proust she generally
carried about with her and reply: 'Darling, this place is a mad-
house.'

From time to time Madame Mère would leave the dining-
room and go into the kitchen, which was on the same floor. This
was a vast, gloomy, perpetually smoke-filled place. Most of the
working space was taken up by a dresser on which things had
been piling up since 1904. The ventilation was shocking and the
maids sweated there like miners down the pit. For lunch the
family was relatively punctual. At dinner time, it was another
story. Madame Mère had to take up her post on the first floor
landing, from which her voice could reach down to the ground
floor and up to the second. Clinging to the banisters, like a captain on his bridge, she would summon her troops. Sometimes, the
family came along. But often nobody appeared, and only the
echo of an indignant *merde* answered her call. On such occasions
Madame Mère used to explode, utter threats, lash out at the

furniture with her walking stick, then go back into the dining-room and loose the cord that held the door. The leaf, moved by the sort of coiled spring that might have worked a catapult in the Hundred Years' War, slammed shut with a noise of thunder.

Monsieur Père was the exact opposite of his wife, gentle, dreamy, diffident and absent-minded. He spent his days on the ground floor; that was where, from first thing in the morning, he painted water-colours, read his favourite authors and went out from time to time to take a turn on the lawn. Apart from my mother, his family bored him, and he was a little scared of me. His favourite friends were Athos and Porthos, two gaily coloured bantam cocks that lived perched on the window-sill of his study. Sometimes he would suddenly grip my wrist and try to teach me sinister poems:

> *In my heart there is only a festering wound*
> *Which I no longer tend against adversity . . .*

His afternoons were devoted to his patients. As he saw these only by appointment, and as his appointments were made by his wife over the telephone, in a memorable formula: 'Hullo! Madame Duchesne, doctor, speaking'; as, moreover, she seldom consulted her husband's engagement book and he never consulted her at all, there was sometimes confusion in the waiting-room.

Monsieur Père's speciality, as set forth on the brass plate fixed to the front door, was Nose, Ears and Throat. He frequently prescribed spectacles and occasionally syringed ears. Some days he even performed operations for cataract on old people. These took place in an improvised theatre behind his consulting-room. To operate, he used to put on a white coat over his frock coat. It all seemed rather amateurish; particularly as in extreme cases he was assisted by Madame Mère, who was no trained nurse but who unhesitatingly muzzled herself in a linen mask which, if not sterile, had at least been boiled. Apparently the operations were usually successful. Monsieur Père must have had some skill, and Madame Mère's authority did the rest.

20

Madame Mère was At Home every Friday afternoon. A special parlour was unlocked for the occasion; it smelt musty, and its walls were hung with paintings by Boudin all representing Trouville in the rain, one sky more lowering than the next. My mother, dressed in flowered cretonne and with her hair in a prim bun, would sit down at the piano. Madame Mère sang Mozart between two choking fits. There was talk of the danger of war, of the Dantzig corridor, of Munich, of Daladier, of Georges Bonnet, of Hitler, of petit-beurre biscuits. The maids in long starched aprons filled crystal glasses. Monsieur Père would put in an appearance between a couple of appointments. He was fond of the ladies and had an agreeably roving eye. He would crack sly jokes, tell risqué stories and make improper Latin quotations.

Is there anything in common between my own children, naked on the beach at Saint-Tropez each summer, drinking Coca-Cola and calling everybody *tu*, since they are afraid neither of other people nor of themselves, is there anything in common between these children and the child that I was? They go into cafés to play with slot machines, whereas I used to go to Vespers in the church of Saint-Taurin, escorted by one of the maids. I would day-dream, kneeling on a *prie-Dieu*, with a foot-warmer full of charcoal at my feet. I prayed amid the smell of incense and the sound of music. What is there in common between myself and them? Nothing. There is a break in continuity between the generations of Frenchmen born about the time of the Popular Front and those that have come into the world since the Liberation. It's nothing to do with the bomb or the moon, and it's not just a quarrel between Ancients and Moderns. It's a complete, irreversible change in the whole system of reference. I am conscious of belonging to the tail-end of a nineteenth-century still steeped in humanism. I am one of those who still seek some sort of order, if only within themselves. But those who are now thrusting open the door don't give a damn for order; they are all movement.

My grandparents' splendid house had no lavatories. And so

every morning the maids performed a medieval chore. They lugged down to the river the huge covered enamel buckets containing the excrement of the entire household. I always went with them. Swaying to the rhythm of their steps, the buckets gave out dubious sounds. According to the nature of the sound and the colour of the bucket, the maids would diagnose the internal condition of each member of the family. They laughed as they talked, amid a smell of muck and scented disinfectant.

In all the upper-class houses of the town, where the gardens overlook the river, they used to throw the stuff into the water every day—their shit and piss, their clap and pox and all the rest. This practice did not deter anyone from washing linen in the *lavoirs* of the said river, nor even from cutting and eating the watercress grown in it.

Who will want to remember what Evreux was like before the Second World War? An exquisite and sordid town, half-heartedly divided between the Church and Radical-Socialism, closer to the world of Abel Hermant than to that of Marcel Proust, and about which none the less there hung a certain charm. The whole town drowsed, timidly huddled at the foot of the cathedral: the squat houses of the Rue Saint-Sauveur and the Rue de la Harpe, the high walls, the secret gardens—the home, as it had always been, of my tribe, of my people, its leading citizens, preposterous creatures, cultured fools, enlightened idiots. In Evreux I witnessed the last spasms of the provincial bourgeoisie, that old privileged caste, like an ageing tart still charming in decay, incapable, however, either of defending its own or of asserting the arbitrary rights which it had invented for itself. When the hurricane of war broke out for the second time since the beginning of the century, it blew the whole thing away.

◆

J.J., Jean Jardin, my father, rang up from Paris to announce that he was coming to Evreux for lunch, bringing Baroness Jean de Ménil, one of the three daughters of Conrad Schlumberger, who had invented a method of prospecting for oil by means of electricity.

I waited eagerly for my father. I adored him, but I seldom saw him. On the rare occasions when our paths met he would hold me between his knees and, with a little tortoiseshell comb, tidy my dishevelled hair with rough, tender movements, repeating between clenched teeth: 'What a good-looking fellow it is.' This was in 1939. Thirty years later, when I meet my father at Lipps' near Saint-Germain-des-Près, he still pulls out his comb and I have the utmost difficulty in escaping from this unskilful hairdresser, this ruthless scratcher of ears.

In 1939 my father was thirty-five. He was a 'railwayman', that's to say he was the right-hand man of Raoul Dautry, general manager of French Railways. He was infatuated with a train which, seen either from the front or the back, presented a perfect oval. It could do the Paris–Lyon–Marseilles run at over 140 km. per hour, and was nicknamed the Sausage Train. Dautry was the man who evolved the S.N.C.F. out of the old Rothschild railway system.

Father had promised to be at Evreux by noon. At half-past one, no sign of him. At a quarter to two, a telephone call. He was at Mantes. He had just been listening to the radio at a petrol-filling station; general mobilization was announced. Madame Mère thundered out that Hitler was a megalomaniac. Monsieur Père tried to calm her down with the slogan that was popular at the time: 'mobilization does not mean war'. She retorted by calling him a cretin. From that time on, everyone lived glued to the radio. On 2nd September war was declared; the adventure had begun.

◆

On 4th September I was told that we weren't going back to Paris. Like practically everyone else in France, we began to retreat. This national stampede started in my case at Bernay, Eure, where my father left us, my mother, my brother and myself. My paternal grandparents had a house there with a big shop on the ground

23

floor: *Maison Jardin, Nouveautés*—Drapery and Fancy Goods. Since the death of my great-grandfather Jean Racine, who was a violinist and a well-known razor-sharpener to several European courts, the place had become the embodiment of boredom.

The radio was not encouraging; it announced a German advance which was all the speedier in that the French army remained invisible. A pork butcher whose shop faced *Jardin, Nouveautés* had lengthy discussions in my grandparents' shop with the bailiff of the De Broglie estate. He asserted that the Wehrmacht soldiers made sausages out of children's flesh; of course, this might have been vocational bias.

Two days later, 6th September, Papa turned up at Bernay at the wheel of an American open tourer like something out of a Bogart movie.

'Get cracking, chaps, I've got five thousand people to find lodgings for.'

Eventually I grasped that we were the spearhead of a fantastic exodus, which in turn was to be merged in an even vaster tide of humanity: we were the advance guard for the whole Parisian staff of French Railways with their families, plus tons of typewriters and adding machines, priceless treasures which must not fall into German hands. The whole crowd was bound for Trouville. It was beyond doubt now: since the Germans had taken up arms, the whole of France was making for the beaches.

◆

The tourer was a black Ford, a squat convertible with a dickey at the back. It was rather splendid-looking with its broad running-boards, its headlamps like preserving pans and its spoked wheels.

We drove fast. Papa and Mama were in front. My brother and I were in the dickey, windblown. As the hood was up we could not see the scenery, only the little square of yellowed mica through which we could make out Mother's broad-brimmed hat and Father's narrow-brimmed one.

Suddenly we had to get out. We were at Beaumont-en-Auge,

24

twenty kilometres from Trouville. The little château at which we had just arrived belonged to M. and Mme de Margerie. He was a diplomat; she ran a literary-political salon in Paris, which she had re-established on the Normandy coast and which was as popular as ever. From the start, my mother, my brother and I felt like displaced persons. Father did not realize this. He had a chameleon-like gift for adapting himself to his social surroundings. His intellectual acrobatics exasperated me for a long time, until I came to realize that I had become the same sort of person myself, using the same tricks, my mind constantly on the alert for what could be got out of other people in the way of amusement and interest, rejecting the rest shamelessly. My father and I are made up of the same chromosomes; we drive straight ahead. We are quite capable of crushing anyone who gets in our way. Afterwards, of course, one is sorry; one is sorry but one never stops.

After a brief negotiation Papa persuaded Mme de Margerie to shelter his family in the outbuildings of her château until he had found a roof for us at Trouville. Then he dumped us there and went on to tackle his own overwhelming problems. Right away, things went badly. The Margeries and ourselves did not speak the same language. Maman, Simon and I had, I suppose, what Swiss and Belgians call a French accent, that's to say no accent at all. But the Margeries' way of speaking was half dental, half English. Dental because they thrust their words forward, pressing their tongues against their teeth, and English because they had learnt English. I couldn't speak either English or dental, so I came off badly.

Mme de Margerie called women 'dear' and men 'cher'. Apparently they meant the same thing. I learned much later that this was untrue. The French adjective 'cher', used by itself in addressing some bearded gentleman in pince-nez, is a piece of outmoded snobbery; whereas 'dear', if you're English, is permissible, it has the backing of tradition and suggests monarchy and fog, a huge island floating in a sea of tea.

The Margeries' little château stood back to back with the village church. Its delicious park overlooked the valley of the Auge. I used sometimes to meet our hosts' children there. Diane was my age, snub-nosed and madly attractive. Unfortunately her governess, a withered prude, did everything in her power to keep us apart. Boby, Diane's brother, was a grown-up of thirteen. As he already knew everything and I already knew nothing, how could we communicate? His judgements fascinated me. During a tea-party to which I had been admitted in spite of my awkward manners and my bewildered look, he said to his mother: 'Maman, you're behind the times. The Duke was through with Zizi six months ago.'

Who was Zizi? What duke? I was baffled. Roughly speaking, I may say that I made my entry into society timidly, by the back door, at about six, and my definitive exit through the window, like a thief, at about twenty-five. Small talk, prefabricated sentiments, venomous smiles, tears as a formality, hand-kissing, cholesterol after dinner, the bric-à-brac of conventional ideas, what's done and what's not done, lackeys, queers, polo, prelates, old dames with face-lifts and old boys gone soft: to hell with them all!

At night the whole of France was in darkness. Our little village did not escape the common fate. Fear crept in slowly from everywhere, insidious as fog. Last night, at ten o'clock, Maman fell down in the street; she hurt herself badly and could not get up again. Nobody came to help her; on the contrary, a passer-by gave her a kick in the stomach, taking her for a drunk.

◆

Trouville-Deauville 1969. I have a suite in the Hôtel Royal. I have come to show Jean Gabin a script I've just finished, the script for his next film. I dine with Régine, I lose at the Casino. The hotel porter calls me by my name and the car attendant brings me my little sports car as soon as I stick my nose outside. I am enveloped and clad in my social persona. I'm the man with several cars, contracts ahead of me, arrears of income tax, shirts made to measure. And yet behind this façade, this plaster and paint—isn't the varnish cracking, as usual? One part of myself looks forward to an uncertain future, the other, turned towards the past, reminds me of the derisory fragility of all this luxury.

Trouville, September 1939. An overcrowded town, at the end of its tether, men who have lost a war they haven't even fought, my father requisitioning lodgings for his railwaymen right and left, even the appalling mid-nineteenth-century Casino. I followed him like a shadow, glad to have him, by a lucky chance, working so near at hand. He tried to go into an hotel, but the porter standing before his door with arms outstretched refused to let in the grimy railwaymen and their families.

'Who's going to pay?'

'You'll be paid like everyone else, when the war is over.'

Peals of aggressive laughter from the porter. Father ordered him to make way. The porter refused. He was a huge man and Father a small one. What triggered it off? The tenseness of the atmosphere, the lack of sleep? My father's head struck the huge paunch with a dull, distressing sound. The fat man toppled over backwards into the revolving door of his establishment.

Delighted by this decisive blow, the railwaymen and their families took the hotel by storm. Half an an hour later the fat man, who had a weak heart, nearly died of retrospective shock.

My father was summoned before a magistrate.

We climbed Mont Canisy, which overlooks Deauville. The bumpy road, which had been patched up with clinkers, crackled like potato crisps under the wheels of the car. A green front door, a horrible shack, a windswept holiday villa in neo-Norman style: the Vert Logis. This was our new home. To crown my misery, in this land where nothing went right there was a school: the Cours Hatemer had been evacuated here. I had to go to it. But being unable to read or count or even tell the time, I could do nothing there except die of boredom. The schoolmistress, a frowstily virtuous bony creature, came to talk to my mother about my desperate case. But my mother refused to be disheartened. In her view, one could learn about life without passing the Certificat d'Études or going to the École Polytechnique. She explained to the teacher that she read Proust and Babar to me and this was enough to awaken my imagination. On hearing this, the 'evacuated' schoolmistress hardened instantly. She took a dislike to me. And I took a loathing to her.

I lived with my mother in a world where Tarzan had married the Duchesse de Guermantes, and this world of mine was incompatible with reality. I detested my schoolfellows with their runny noses, their scratched knees, their marbles and black pinafores. The image of these children, who were simple-minded and often stupid, sometimes cruel, still haunts me. It was truly at the Cours Hatemer at Blonville that I first began to reject despotism.

'Mademoiselle, I want to be excused.'

'Later on; you must hold it back.'

Why later, why hold it back? And what if I couldn't?

I can still see myself, sweating as I bent over my exercise book, desperately tackling my pothooks. The vision of that cross-ruled exercise book still dances before my eyes. Twenty years later, when I met Vadim while working as Marc Allégret's assistant and discovered that he wrote his film scripts in school exercise books, I felt physically sick.

I have never had any education. My primary school was a big Parisian daily where I was reporter on the entertainments page at the age of twenty-two. My first essay was a 'close-up' study of an unknown actor, Yul Brynner. My first and only distinction was a bonus of 200 francs offered by the editors for having collaborated with the journalist Yves Salgues in a series of articles on 'What Kruschev blames Stalin for'. And yet I had written so much nonsense in it, and so had Salgues, that after the publication of the tenth article Boris Souvarine, an eminent specialist in Soviet affairs, came to tell the editor-in-chief that we ought to be in a mental home. On which Salgues had told me: 'Don't worry, I'm Russian.' 'From what region?' 'From the Lot.'

Thus began a passionate if stormy friendship. Having learnt

to read at fifteen, I had and I still have a highly idiosyncratic spelling. Salgues corrected my mistakes, and I passed on my girl friends to him, when he took it into his head that they were prettier than his own.

Yves Salgues is a colossus with a bonnetful of bees. He's a madman who has lost everything except his wits. For a long time he reigned over the woman's weekly *Jours de France*. He earned his living by dipping his vitriolic pen in honey, relating with discreet enthusiasm the pregnancies of queens, the marriages of Bardot. His mind is full of strange streaks, and he tends to speak in melodious alexandrines. His brain teems with chimerical fancies, and the slightest of his explanations is as dense and luxuriant as the Amazonian forest: thus for him Marcel Dassault is not the colossal industrialist that everyone knows, but 'a vegetarian Venetian potentate in wrinkled woollen socks, who may be short-sighted but can see all the further for it'. He lives with a stray dog I gave him, which, against all odds, he has managed to make his legal heir. He sings bits of Dos Passos as others might sing Charles Trenet. I love his erotic tales with their high-powered pornography, about ladies in Dordogne castles with inordinate appetites and grandiose charms, who piss after making love and belch after eating. Yves Salgues, my oldest friend and my toughest enemy. The man who first betrayed me, and who taught me that the battle of Paris has to be fought every morning. This journalist of genius trained me and corrupted me. I learned from him that crazy resilience that keeps one up-to-date. I remember that at dawn, when the first edition had been printed, we would come home on foot, stopping at every bar. His inexhaustible verve poured down his cheeks like the beer he drank. 'Beware of dawn, it's the time when the corpses of drowned Rastignacs land up like collapsed puppets at Police Headquarters.' Whatever he may have done, I keep him in a special place in the twilight zone of my secret, unexplained and inexplicable friendships.

At that time I was not Yves Salgues' only assistant. There were three of us. The first of my colleagues was a film critic and a conscientious objector. He would take refuge by day at Louise de Vilmorin's and hand in his implacable articles at night, when policemen are asleep. He was François Truffaut. The second was a thin, stuttering Swiss, dim-sighted behind dirty sun-glasses; he was already known as Godard. He had not yet become the visionary author of *A bout de souffle* and *Pierrot le Fou*. His whole face wore the impotent and costive look often displayed by budding creators striving to give birth to powerful expression.

◆

Late October 1939. My father took me to visit Jean Schlumberger at the château of Val-Richer, near Lisieux. This was a huge early seventeenth-century building, where everything reminded one that Guizot had lived there. On the edge of the estate was a Renaissance manor-house, Braffy, where Jean Schlumberger had given shelter to the writer Joseph Breibach.

One doesn't live one's life in the right order. It's surely a mistake to start with childhood.

For indeed that day I knew nothing. I didn't know that Jean Schlumberger was one of the founders of the *Nouvelle Revue Française*, nor that he was a close friend of Joseph Breibach, nor that when I was twenty I should marry the daughter of the publisher Jean Fayard and come here on my honeymoon, nor that in 1943 my father was to save Breibach from the Gestapo by pretending he was a Cuban tobacco expert, nor that in 1954, out of gratitude to my father, Breibach would hand over to the penniless, homeless young married man that I was the keys of a flat he no longer used in the Rue du Val-de-Grâce. I could not tell that in this flat, being on my own one summer's night in Paris, I was to become the lover of my future second wife, and that surprised by the maid, one of the earliest Portuguese immigrants, I should offer the panic-stricken explanation: 'It's all right, she's my sister.'

It was in this flat, too, that I quarrelled with my godfather, the wealthy Catholic writer Daniel-Rops, whose real name was Petiot.

He disinherited me because I had become the assistant and friend of the film producer Marc Allégret, the hero of André Gide's *Journal*.

Marc's destiny has been a strange one. Son of a Protestant minister in Basel, a wayward private dreamer, well-bred to the very depths of his being, he has been the greatest talent-scout of the French cinema. His films have always proved spring-boards for their script-writers and their actors. Jean-Pierre Aumont, Simone Simon, Fresnay, Darrieux, Bardot, Gelin, Delon, Belmondo, Annie Girardot, Jacques Prévert, Anouilh, Vadim, all of them have passed through his hands. Some of them he may even be said to have invented. And yet all of them without exception have got away from him, or rather he ceased caring for them once they had become famous. He no longer knew what to do with them. The life of Marc Allégret is like that of a ferryman who secretly picks up unknown people, carries them into the light and goes back into the darkness alone, quite alone, without complaining, without even really ceasing to smile.

•

If I had not visited the château of Val-Richer at the end of 1939 the whole subsequent course of my life would have been different. I should never have become acquainted with that Protestant network which indirectly led me, one day, to work in the cinema. And I should never have seen the unfinished jigsaw puzzle with three thousand pieces that took up a whole sitting-room, nor, up in the attic, those old bath-tubs full of electric wire in which Conrad Schlumberger made his first experiments in prospecting the subsoil by means of electricity. Today, thanks to him, his grandchildren are part-owners of the town of Houston, Texas, and collect royalties on every barrel of the black gold that goes out into the world.

•

December 1939. Winter had come. Deauville and its beach were deserted. The roadsweepers had gone to the war and the wind drove the sand right up behind the Casino.

One grey, rainy, typically Norman morning we found the gas and electricity cut off. We had to leave Blonville. We took refuge at Trouville, in the little Chatham Hotel facing the sea, some thirty metres from the Casino where Father had installed his offices. In the evenings, when all his customers had left, M. Bestrer, the owner of the hotel (he had once been manager of the London Ritz) told us his adventures. Almost all the lights in the bar were out. I drank orangeade through a straw and listened, terrified:

'The bastard was at the end of the corridor and I'd got him at the end of my Lüger.'

'What's a Lüger?'

'An automatic pistol, my lad . . .'

•

The telephone service was not functioning. Only those people who had high-up administrative jobs could use it. We were having our family meal one evening when the maître d'hôtel informed my father that Lieutenant Pierre Laudenbach wanted to speak to him. This unfortunate officer was desperately anxious to inform his captain by telephone that, all means of transport being paralysed, it was physically impossible for him to rejoin his regiment.

I shall never forget the entry of Lieutenant Laudenbach into the hotel dining-room. And yet I had never seen *La Grande Illusion*. Now that I know the film by heart I realize that at Trouville that evening I saw Captain de Boïeldieu in the flesh, with his puttees and his noble unassuming air. It was Pierre Fresnay.

He was accompanied not by Von Stronheim but by his wife, Yvonne Printemps. She was beautiful, with a slender boyish figure, a cascade of golden hair, a prickly character, a comical turned-up nose and a voice whose incomparable modulations were like smiles.

I loved both of them on the spot. They belonged, they still belong to the race of impossible people. He was as solid as a sea wall against which his wife's fantastic fits of temper were endlessly breaking. 'The actor Fresssnay', she would call him, teasingly disdainful, avidly tender. He was her thing. And she liked to say: 'If you only knew how handsome he was when I took him.' It was like a game, a kind of war between them. I know now that for him it is a holy war and that he has never surrendered.

I know only two men who treasure their wives so highly: Pierre Fresnay and myself. But he has one enormous advantage over me: his marriage has gone on longer. In 1939 he worshipped Yvonne Printemps unconditionally. In 1959, when I was writing a film script for Fresnay and Darry Cowl, I saw that his passion had not cooled. Finally, a few months ago, I went to see him after the show at the Théâtre de la Michodière where he had revived *Le Neveu de Rameau*. I drove back with him from the theatre to his home in Neuilly. I have never been so frightened in my life. He scorched through Paris at nearly 140 kilometres an hour and tore past three red lights. All this to get back three minutes sooner to his wife.

I have heard it said that these two were held together by some artifice. I don't agree at all with that explanation. To my mind, only love could have lasted so long.

◆

Until April 1940 it was the phoney war. Frenchmen and Germans stared at one another without fighting. I had stopped going to school. I hung about on the beach. The electricity had come back and we returned to the Vert Logis at Blonville. In the evenings, in the ice-cold house, I used to drink hot spiced wine and listen to records of Mistinguett on a gramophone given us by the proprietor of the Chatham at Trouville.

On 10th May the Germans attacked. On the 14th, my birthday, they bombed Le Havre. The huge oil depots in the harbour were set ablaze. The fire lasted for eight days and eight nights. From my bedroom window I gazed for hours at this gigantic, limitless furnace. In the morning the mist seemed to damp down the brilliance of the flames. But at night the town blazed like the very torch of war. I was obsessed by the thought of my own death, but without distress. My preoccupations were purely concrete. I asked my mother whether angels had adjustable wings. I packed a little suitcase to take to Heaven. I prayed a good deal.

My father, apprehensive on our behalf of a general bombard-ment of the Normandy coast, evacuated us yet again. He bought a cottage like Snow-White's further inland, at Bourgeauville, above Houlgate. This dream cottage proved uninhabitable. Re-gretfully, we went to stay with a fat farmer's wife some hundred metres away. Soon bread ran short. Then the butcher departed. One day we woke up to find outselves in a deserted village. Trouville was empty too. It looked as if the plague had ravaged it. The few remaining inhabitants went into abandoned shops to help themselves. A horde of dogs had been left behind and they howled dismally. Old folk who could not be moved waited on their doorsteps for heaven knows what. Who fed them, who looked after them? This was the backlash of Verdun, the reverse of the Chemin des Dames. This time we had not lost one million five hundred thousand men. But at what a cost: forty million Frenchmen were shitting their pants at the same time. It makes a revolting noise in my memory.

◆

My father was ordered to withdraw into Vendée immediately with his railwaymen. He requisitioned every vehicle he could lay hands on, from Rolls-Royces to pig-trucks. We took the lead of this odd caravan in a huge coffee-coloured Peugeot with folding seats, called Sofica. Towns were empty, roads were crowded. The whole of France, as tireless as ourselves, was taking to its heels. Fugitives encountered whole armies, apparently in full flight. In the fields one saw abandoned suitcases and pieces of furniture. People fought like animals for five litres of petrol. In the farms, peasants whose resources were exhausted had to barricade themselves against refugee families, ready to kill to get food for their children.

Saint-Jean-de-Monts was the obligatory end of our journey. You couldn't go any further except by swimming. At the sea's edge the pine trees grew out of the sand. The farms were low and squat, the better to resist the wind. The town was full to bursting. We settled in as best we could, all four of us, in a room in the Hôtel de l'Espérance.

My mother took me for walks in the gorse-covered dunes. We visited Clemenceau's house. I struck up a passionate friendship with the hotel-owner's Saint Bernard. He had the bloodshot eyes of an alcoholic. I loved his shaggy, incurable mournful face. I made room for him in my bed.

One afternoon when we were alone together, wanting to demonstrate his affection for me, he stood up on his hind legs and leaned against me. I fell over backwards and the dog's claws scraped my face. I couldn't see out of my left eye and my face was streaming with blood; I called for help. They came, they grabbed the dog as though he were a refractory convict, they struck him in spite of my protests and finally passed sentence on him. Judged guilty by a jury of waitresses, cooks and evacuated bourgeois, he was condemned to death. Despite my cries, his master slaughtered him in the courtyard of the hotel.

I became a pessimist. I was to remain one.

I clearly remember the faces of the jurymen who condemned that innocent Saint Bernard to death. They all looked decent people.

Sods' faces from time immemorial, eyes inexpressive to the point of vacancy, coarse mouths that could eat but not taste, that spoke without understanding, that spewed out nonsense. They are always the same. When they die they are resurrected. They will last as long as the earth lasts. You meet them everywhere: inquisitors, screws, beaks, sneaks, censors, bullies, Gestapists, purgers, or worse still, acquiescent spectators. They will always be ready to accuse someone, even if it's only a dog.

*

16th June. A gloomy lunchtime. In the dining-room of the over-full hotel, extreme tension prevailed. At three o'clock the loudspeaker of the radio announced that Marshal Pétain was going to make a solemn appeal. Everyone stood up: 'Men and women of France, from today I shall take over the leadership of the French government . . .' As he spoke, faces froze . . .'Last night I approached our adversary to ask, as between soldiers, whether he was prepared to join with us, after the battle and in all honour, in bringing an end to hostilities . . .' And then many people started crying, standing there crowded together in that seaside hotel dining-room. A very old gentleman who had been unable to get to his feet crumpled up and hid his face in his hands. My father was white as a sheet. I asked him what had happened. He answered softly:

'We have lost the war.'

*

20th June. Four o'clock in the afternoon. I was on the beach in my swimsuit, with my mother. I was still expecting death, with an optimistic thirst for the unknown which I was soon to get over. A noise from the sky set a wind of panic blowing. It was a swastika'ed fighting plane. It flew low over the beach. An old gentleman shook his fist at it and spat on the ground, yelling: 'A Messerschmitt!'

Five o'clock. I heard cries. I saw a woman come running up, carrying her baby. Three motor-cycles rode up on to the beach. The riders wore boots and helmets and tight green uniforms. They had tommy-guns slung round their necks. The motor-bikes swooped down on to the sand. They stopped close by me, three metres away from the water's edge. Everybody stood silent.

I stared hard at the three soldiers. They were quite young, and spoke in loud shouting voices. The one who seemed to be the leader gave an order. The other two started up their machines again and drove off alongside the water, one to the left, the other to the right. The leader looked at the sea for a moment; he must have been about twenty.

Now the town was full of noise. The tanks came in. They were huge, pot-bellied, dirty grey. They left the marks of their caterpillar wheels in the hot tarmac. They were all armed with guns, the tips of which were covered with leather cases. The French watched them without saying a word. From the turret of each there emerged a German, naked to the waist. They were mostly fair-haired and all young. With incredible speed they pitched their tents in the dunes and drew up the tanks and trucks in close ranks. One of them gave me a piece of chocolate. A gentleman snatched it from me and flung it into the gutter. After dinner the Germans filed past, marching rhythmically and singing *Aie-i Aie-O Aia*. I said to my brother that it was a nice tune. A lady boxed my ears.

◆

24th June. A telephone call from Saintes, ordering my father to get back to Trouville with his railwaymen at all costs. All the adding machines of the S.N.C.F. had been left in the Casino. Unless they were retrieved very fast the Germans were likely to seize them. After that he must return to Paris at top speed, otherwise the head offices of the Railways might be taken over.

So we set off again. This time the roads were crowded with everybody going home, plus the Germans. Bridges had been blown up all over the place. Papa had to argue for an hour with a German officer, who eventually agreed to let the convoy of railwaymen through. In the end we crossed the Loire on a bridge made of rubber rafts.

At Trouville it was not the Germans but the hotel proprietors who, not having been paid, refused to hand over the adding machines. There were more arguments and more scuffles. This time my father did not threaten anyone, and we got back to Paris with all the equipment.

◆

End of November 1940. Paris was grey and cold and dirty. In the streets there were few people and few cars. Café windows had been painted blue. People slunk by, hugging the walls. There were Germans everywhere. Defeat had taken over.

I no longer went to school and, what's more, I was taken to the theatre. I saw Jean Anouilh's *Léocadia*, played by Yvonne Printemps and Pierre Fresnay.

I remember very little about the play but a great deal about my own excitement: arriving at the theatre, where the curtain went up at seven p.m. because of the curfew; the darkened hall, the three taps, Yvonne singing *Les chemins qui mènent à la mer*, an old taxi appearing on the stage and then, after the performance, my first visit to the other side of the footlights, a journey through the wings, and there, a monstrous revelation: the taxi that I'd seen come on to the stage was not a real taxi but merely the plywood silhouette of a motor-car.

That night I discovered illusion. The idea that a car might be nothing but a façade, the idea that Yvonne Printemps shed make-believe tears, that Pierre Fresnay had pretended to comfort her and that we spectators had pretended to believe them. It was only one step from there to thinking that invention was better than reality. Later I was to take another, when I learned deliberately to confuse invention and lies and to reject reality as far as possible in favour of organized fantasy. Gradually I came to make practical use of my capacity for dreaming, until the day when I finally succeeded in becoming entirely a spectator of my own life, a *voyeur*, an author.

That evening at the Théâtre de la Michodière, above the wings, in Yvonne's dressing-room, there actually was an author, the author of the play. The interesting thing is that he had the authentic look of an author, the look that all true playwrights ought to have, the look of somebody who is to be buried hugger-mugger,

38

without the rites of Mother Church, the look of a *voyeur* who has spied, through the keyhole, on hell making love with heaven.

I do not know Jean Anouilh, except by sight. But three days ago, in a café in the Place de l'Alma, thirty years after that first occasion, I found myself sitting opposite him. I watched him talking to the actress Francine Bergé. An expression of acute, overwhelming consternation pervaded his clerkly features, and behind his round glasses there gleamed two terrible eyes that seemed to look only into the depths of himself.

◆

January 1941. I longed to travel. I thought death might be a journey. At home I met Arletty; her beauty bowled me over, but to no purpose. I was small, incurably small. However violently I rejected this inferior status, there was no help for it. I was still a child, that's to say a creature possessing nothing at all, neither house nor car nor love nor liberty.

My father had just been appointed Principal Private Secretary to Yves Bouthillier, Minister of Finance.

I knew the Louvre that we visited on half-holidays to see the Mona Lisa; now I became precociously acquainted with that other Louvre in the Rue de Rivoli, the seat of fiscal power.

I often went with Mother to fetch Father at his office, which had a balcony adorned with statues overlooking the gardens. They introduced me to the Minister. He was a slender white-haired man, with a calm resolute expression. But what surprised me most was not the Minister but his study. It was huge, with curtains made of white brocade studded with golden fleurs-de-lys. Much later, I was to visit it again one evening to fetch Antoine Pinay* and take him out to dinner with Jean Gabin. There was a memorable conversation, which began with the greatest courtesy:

'Monsieur Gabin, I have seen you in films.'

* Prime Minister 1952. De Gaulle's finance minister 1958–60. Now *médiateur* or Ombudsman at the age of eighty-three.

'Monsieur le Président, I have seen you on television.'

'Your latest picture is a great success.'

'But your loan is a triumph.'

That evening Gabin had put aside that living language invented wholly by himself, derived from the ring, from the Navy, from bars, from the cycle-racing track, from the Parisian faubourgs, from his association with Jacques Prévert, his love affair with Marlene Dietrich, his long collaboration with Michel Audiard. He had sifted that prodigious gritty flow of language so as to keep out all preposterous inventions, all surrealist images. He had simply talked about the education of his daughters. That evening, at Taillevent's restaurant, he was no longer Pépé le Moko but a powerful and lonely man, questioning himself after a tough life.

When dinner was over President Pinay confided to me in astonishment: 'I expected to be dining with an actor, not with a *grand bourgeois!*'

I could not quite explain to him the multiple personality of Jean Gabin. He had dined with the hero of *Les Grandes Familles*, with the Clemenceau of *Le Président*, dressed to perfection, wearing a princely collar and tie. Only that particular Gabin, with his tricolour appearance—red face, blue eyes, white hair—that Gabin with his right hand slightly curved in an accusing gesture, is never more than a part of the whole man. I know other Gabins: the nomad, who is forever moving with his family from one home to another, taking all his furniture with him, like a seventeenth-century nobleman. I know the very great actor, thoughtful and yet wholly instinctive, superstitious and psychic. I know the anarchist, a sort of aristocrat in a cloth cap who moves like a cat, thinks things that nobody else thinks and speaks Gabin as you might speak English. That anarchical fellow conforms to no standards, and if I call him an aristocrat it is because whatever emanates from him owes nothing to anybody. I know Gabin the misanthrope, the pessimist, the misogynist, who regards two-thirds of humanity as swine and the other third as fools, who thinks that Europe is done for and that the 'yellow men' are going to checkmate us, who considers nearly all women to be butches, bitches and witches and compares Lesbians to highly suspect snake-charmers. I know Gabin the epicurean, who thinks that since life is a long journey one ought to travel first class; the unhappy, anguished Gabin who has always been racked by the thought of death and who has often repeated to me the inscription which, as a child, he read on a tombstone: 'None ever knows the day nor the hour.' And I also know the timid, secretive and prudish Gabin, who has never changed his shirt in front of a colleague, who is incapable of telling anyone clearly that he thinks well of them, who did not know how children were born until he was sixteen, who started as a manual worker at the age of thirteen, whose father was a dissolute actor, who had no mother, whose childhood was partly crushed and who bears within himself unhealed wounds. This retired seducer has unsuspected reticences about everything connected with personal emotions. He always says he loves nobody. I don't believe that is true.

♦

Paris 1941 meant cold and hunger, air-raid warnings every night and the shelter in the cellar under the rod-of-iron rule of our foul concierge, who had the rank of chief air-raid warden. My father decided to send his family out of Paris, to his parents' home at Bernay, for greater safety.

So we set off again for that dreary provincial town, while I longed for a different one—for Evreux. Maman, Simon and I settled in over my grandparents' shop, *Jardin, Nouveautés*.

Smashing open a recalcitrant secret drawer I found a gold coin, a *louis d'or*. My grandfather took it from me and opened an account in my name at the Savings Bank. Wild with rage, I vowed to my mother that I would never save a single penny. More's the pity!

Under pressure from my right-minded grandparents, Mother sent me to school with my brother. I stayed there two days and then took myself off. They caught me, and I was promptly sent as day-boarder to a Catholic institution. Here there were regular hours for working and eating and peeing. It was hell. I rejected it. A frenzied thirst for living possessed me, which I was never to lose. I fought back, I tried to kick over the traces with all the energy of despair. I knew that if I gave in, if I joined the rank and file of the poor little dimwits and walked in the long school crocodile on a Thursday afternoon I would lose my chance of the life I longed for, a life outside society. So I wet my bed, I cried for no reason, I drank wine on the sly, I behaved like a little hooligan, I belched and farted in the face of my horrified relatives. All these unruly manifestations of despair made a dreadful impression on the bourgeoisie of Bernay. I was mad, depraved, a juvenile delinquent. They pointed at me in the street. The thought of not being like other people reassured me a bit. My only refuge was my mother. She alone could see what I was trying to become. She alone could see that I was struggling to save myself from drowning. Because of the support she gave me, she incurred my grandparents' disapproval. In order to save my soul in jeopardy, they sent me to catechism class. I happened on a priest who was a joker and liked jazz; he drew me into his confessional in the hope of exorcising me.

I have a pleasant memory of my first confession. The darkness, the confined space, the priest's whispering voice with its hint of complicity, the guarantee of temporary impunity, the mental luxury that ensued, the generosity of pardon and the relief of absolution, with just one Lord's Prayer by way of penitence—it was wonderful. Later, my relations with the clergy deteriorated. For if to begin with the Cross inspired wild hope, the holy-water-sprinkler very soon gave me the creeps. Then I became suspicious of cassocks. I mistrusted these men dressed like mourning women; what were they, God's lady friends? My twice-weekly catechism classes bewildered me; the threats of hell-fire gave me nightmares. And then, if Christ was a Jew, why was the whole parish anti-Semitic? Why were we all summoned to pray and fast and behave well to no purpose, since in the end only a few would be chosen?

42

My latent anguish about the hereafter has never been allayed by the paraphernalia of piety nor by vaguely socialistic jamborees. Even now, when the fancy takes me to go into a church—the other day for instance into the Romanesque Abbey of Saint-Jouin-de-Marnes, in Poitou, it was eleven o'clock on a Sunday morning—what did I see and hear there, in that regal, mystical, austere, military, inspired place? A hesitant driveller play-acting the Mass in French to his audience, interpolating an insipid sermon, devoid of any force of expression, devoid of greatness of any sort, devoid of the slightest passion, lukewarmly pro-Vietnam, very vaguely pro-Trade Union. Bossuet is dying, Bossuet is dead. Long live Guy Lux!*

•

One fine morning the monotony of my life was broken by a German who requisitioned the room next to mine. Panic prevailed throughout the house; a great to-do, forced smiles. At lunch my terrified grandparents, in lowered voices, repeated the touching, dusty old legend of my great-grandmother who in 1870 kept a haberdashery at Bernay. The Duke of Mecklenburg having been assassinated by a Frenchman on the Broglie road, there were reprisals, and the town was bombarded. A cannon ball passed so close to the spire of Notre-Dame-de-la-Couture that it has been crooked ever since. The cannon fire made a great deal of noise but did little damage, and the inhabitants assumed they were out of danger when, suddenly, my great-grandmother saw three Prussians on horseback outside her shop. She rushed off to find her husband's sporting rifle and threw it, fully loaded and butt foremost, down the vast hole of the lavatory. Ever since then people have lived in fear of the gun going off and peppering someone's backside.

My grandparents' German lodger looked like a poor, timid young man. The look was deceptive. Three days after his arrival he entertained two friends. They drank themselves sick, brayed

* French telly-personality; symbol of banality.

43

like asses, played Russian roulette, didn't quite succeed in killing themselves but broke the furniture, knocked in the walls, smashed the mirrors and completely ruined a huge cherry-wood bed by jumping on it—there was no holding them. It was pandemonium!

My ordeal at Bernay lasted until 1st April 1942, when my father was appointed Principal Private Secretary to Robert Gibrat, Minister of Public Works, and when, for some reason that nobody can remember, he brought his family back to Paris.

Father's new Minister was a caricature of an egghead. He had been top of the list on his entry to the Polytechnique and top of the list on graduating from it. He was the inventor of a system known as 'tidal power'. The principle is an attractive one, with a touch of fantasy. When the tide rises it fills enormous tanks. When it ebbs, the emptying of the tanks sets in action turbines which make electricity. The advantage of power stations of this sort is twofold: first, they have to be built on the seashore, which is surely pleasanter than the outer suburbs; secondly, they can't break down unless the moon should suddenly go on strike. The Ministry of Public Works functioned in a fine house formerly belonging to Count Louis Mathieu Molé, 219 Boulevard Saint-Germain. It had a shady garden where I bowled my hoop.

My father's brilliant appointment in no wise solved the horrible problem of my schooling. Since I could not go to a school where children knew how to work, I was forcibly thrust into a sort of private kindergarten, ultra-fashionable, patronised by the wife of a Protestant banker, Mme Fauchier-Delavigne. (The name, as my parents' friend Jean Aurenche pointed out, suggests a very curious imperative.*) This little gilded cage was situated in the Rue Las Cases, just opposite our home. On the very first day I found a party going on there. Possibly to cock a snook at rationing, all the children were dressed as vegetables. I was forcibly disguised as a leek, in green crêpe paper. I wept with humiliation.

A little prune of my own age with a gipsy look about her made fun of me and teased me with spiteful pinches. This horrible

* Faut chier de la vigne: must shit some vine.

44

child was the daughter of our friend and neighbour, Professor René Sauvage, one of the pioneers of thoracic surgery, grandson of Frédéric Sauvage, a perpetually debt-ridden physicist who had invented the screw propeller and its nautical uses. This singular character, who died insane, had discovered the language of spiders and used to tame them in the prisons where his creditors periodically had him thrown. The little prune with her mixed Creole, Italian and Hungarian gipsy blood, whose French Protestant ancestors had emigrated to Puerto Rico on the revocation of the Edict of Nantes, looked at me with piercing eyes. She was later to become the object of my obsessions, the axis round which my whole life revolves, my second wife. She had a name which might have come straight out of Claudel's *L'Annonce faite à Marie*: Stéphane-Marie Sauvage.

◆

My father and mother often left Paris for a few days; and my brother Simon and I were left in the care of a woman to whom I shall give a fictitious name, the only one in this book: Florence.

Florence meant my first plunge into the unknown, a window opening on to the unconscious, the dizzying discovery of relations other than those commonly considered acceptable and rational; the indelible imprint of a certain physical appearance and style, of unfamiliar gestures. With Florence I began to learn that behind the usual meaning of words there lay another, or several others. She was not really beautiful; a redhead, thirtyish, sexy. She had no training and no money. My mother came to her rescue and found her a job as housekeeper to Professor Sauvage. Her shocking temper eventually got her dismissed from that hospitable home. It was then that she came to live with us. At this period, and despite my entreaties, my brother had surrendered to the common fate. He went to school every day. So I was left alone with Florence. To begin with, our relations were unexceptional. She was the friend, the governess, I was the little boy. Soon her para-maternal attitude towards me changed. She became

45

irritable, and yet I suspected that she was not really irritated. She became tyrannical, not after the fashion of a spiteful woman but as though she took a special interest in me, an interest which she tried to make me understand without being able to explain it. After a few weeks she made me bring her breakfast in bed. There was the smell of a tawny wild animal about her and this disturbed me. The careful and calculated injustice, mingled with tenderness, of her behaviour towards me disquieted me extremely. She talked to me a great deal. She asserted that the physical freedom my mother let me enjoy was harmful to my education. She was convinced that a child needed discipline. I began to expect something, I didn't quite know what. One day she slapped me for no reason. It was only a slight blow, but it staggered and terrified me. Why did she hit me? In the end I asked her. She didn't answer; she kissed me.

As time went by she took to striking me with increasing frequency, although never savagely. Realizing that she probably wanted to make me cry, I cried; and then we drifted together into a tunnel of bizarre tenderness in which kisses seemed to be the necessary consequence of the violence that had preceded them. Days flowed by like dreams. A hundred times during the course of a day I would pass from hot to cold, from gaiety to misery. Basically, I was her lover.

After much hesitation, I suppose, she allowed me to meet my rival. I would never be jealous of him, probably, because her relations with men were intangible; there was nothing I could get hold of. He was a young Austrian officer, a film producer temporarily attached to the propaganda film service of the Wehrmacht in Paris. He spoke perfect French, and we became fond of one another. When he first started coming to our house Florence and he used to send me to play in my own room. But gradually I found myself becoming a third party to their private relationship. I had the feeling that they were acting a play. It never varied. Everything seemed to have been laid down once and for all. He would arrive carrying presents. She would accept them, always very scantily clad and wearing tall, high-heeled

46

boots of fine black kid from Perugia's. After exchanging a few anodyne remarks they would go into the drawing-room. She would sit down on a round pouffe and cross her legs so as to display her muscular thighs. He would sit on the ground at her feet and present his gifts. She would examine them meticulously and then, after pauses during which time and life seemed to stop, she would slap his face or give him a kick, without getting up, just with a sharp thrust of her leg. He never spoke a word. His wide-open eyes seemed to stare out at an unfamiliar world. I had the impression not merely that I was not embarrassing them but that I was being of use to them.

I never saw them make love. Did they really do so, or did this mysterious performance serve as substitute for everything?

One day I learned that he had been sent to the front to film battles and had been killed there. I had lost my first friend, the first man with whom I had really shared a secret.

His death brought me even closer to Florence. I never breathed a word to anyone about the way she behaved towards me. Until I was grown up I never even told my mother, although she is a person who does not pass judgement. I must have been aware that if I spoke I would get into trouble and would end up alone again. I was right. They would have parted us. She would have been condemned as a sadist, an exhibitionist, a monster who was making a little masochist of me—three very elementary terms to describe the network of unformulated bonds that united me to her. One can't be a sadist in isolation; an accomplice, an ally is needed. I was that docile, mute partner, not understanding and yet participating. I was neither happy nor unhappy, but I was alive at last.

Florence has remained my point of reference in sensual matters. Although she did not succeed in teaching me to take pleasure in pain, she imprinted deep within me a powerful sexual response to the attraction of boots. My first sexual desire was aroused by this redhead's plump shapely legs in high elegant boots, and I know that if tomorrow I should meet a girl I fancied wearing boots, something within me would beat faster; not only in my body but also in my heart.

47

By way of symbol and token, I'll mention that shortly after our marriage my first wife began refusing to wear boots to please me. For me this was the beginning of an irreversible process of defeat. I was incapable of winning over a being who shared my life, and of making her really accept something which was more than just a personal taste for me but a means to an end, a way of approach, of communication. It meant, finally, that I was incapable of taking her out of herself and bringing her into contact with me.

There are no details in the alchemy which inclines one human being towards another. To her mind, wearing boots meant having to assume a certain appearance in order to attract me. My weakness put her in an uneasy position which deprived her of her identity. She could no longer recognize herself in relation to me. She felt a mere object. And for my own part I could not understand how anyone could refuse to make a gesture.

One gesture after another being refused, we gradually reached a deadlock which proved one day to be paralysis. And by the time I got divorced I felt nothing. The limb that had been amputated was already lifeless.

My second wife brought me boots, and also freedom of movement and of thought. Sheer freedom. She dispersed my obsessions as the wind drives away smoke, while yet allowing them to glow on under the embers. With her, I have found my holy war. With her, I am learning to live every day. We tear one another to pieces, but we rebuild one another. Not side by side but face to face, brow against brow, ruthlessly, like bulls.

◆

20th April 1942. My father was appointed Principal Private Secretary to the Prime Minister, Pierre Laval. We left Paris, taking Florence with us. I was never again to be alone with her. Our adventure was over.

Today, on consulting the calendar and checking the date of my father's appointment, I note that I came back from Bernay to Paris on 1st April 1942 and left again on 21st April. This means that all I had lived through, my partnership with the young officer, his disappearance, his death, the new experiences which made my head explode, happened within a mere three weeks. How had I found time to move so fast?

Our departure meant a retreat towards babyhood for me. After being suddenly flung upwards into unknown regions I was now moving backwards.

The car in which we undertook this new excursion was a big Panhard with its steering wheel almost in the centre of the dashboard. The road had changed a lot since the exodus. It was empty, all ours. Father drove like a madman. We flashed through Moulins like meteors. Apparently in these days the faster one went the safer one was.

Lying down in the back seat I watched the telegraph poles speed past. I felt sick. Everything was a muddle; where were we going? To the Prime Minister's office?

'Maman, why isn't it in Paris?'

'Because Paris is in the occupied zone, darling.'

'And what's Vichy in?'

'In the free zone, darling.'

'But why Vichy?'

'Because Vichy's in the centre, darling.'

'The centre of what?'

'Of France, darling.'

The wheels rolled on. I got bored. Florence was remote; she seemed to be dreaming of somewhere else. Simon was methodically removing the tiny pebbles that had collected in the ribbed soles of his rubber boots. We went through a village: on the right was a big house, the Château de Charmeil, where Marshal Pétain lived. One kilometre further on was another, smaller château, ours.

We drove up a dirt road and through one gate, then another, and drew up in front of a long low building, with one upper floor and a gently sloping roof. The walls were covered with pale brown roughcast. In front of the house was a terrace edged with

D

box, three metres wide, overlooking a meadow where a circus pony, abandoned by its owners during the débâcle, was performing brilliant feats for its own amusement. Behind the house lay a tennis court invaded by weeds, a pond full of frogs and a lofty barn beyond which stood the farm with its outhouses.

The inside of the building smelt of dried fruit gone musty. We settled in haphazardly, as best we could. Mother unpacked our cases. I put my gramophone on the billiard-table in the huge living-room. And this austere residence, the home of a lawyer from Cusset, rang with the voice of Mistinguett: '*Il m'a vue nue, plus que nue, toute nue . . .*' I discovered a study whose walls were hung with gloomy portraits, crazed with age like jigsaw puzzles. They were the lawyer's ancestors. Simon and I tried out our new set of darts on these Auvergnat worthies. In less than a week we had turned them from fossils into colanders.

◆

Stones went whistling past my ears. Suddenly Titi gave a fearful shriek and dropped his gun. He was holding his left hand to his right eye. Gradually his fingers became covered with blood. I examined him; he'd been lucky, his eye was unhurt. Titi was the son of the village carpenter. We had been friends since the moment I came to Charmeil. He made catapults, guns that would shoot stones. He carved the butts and I provided him with the inner tubes of car tyres, out of which we cut strings of elastic. They were dangerous weapons, they could shoot stones as big as pigeons' eggs a distance of thirty metres. My brother was the leader of one gang, and I organized another. For the time being my headquarters were in the toolshed. Simon had collected the bulk of his troops close to the pond. His forces were considerable, at least ten fellows whose ages ranged from eight to twelve. The battle had been raging for two hours. I had only six supporters, but my strategic position was better than his.

Simon was bombarding us pitilessly. We could not answer

back, for we only had light weapons. We had to stick it out. His cannon was a wheelbarrow at the front of which two big pieces of wood were fixed with screws. It was an enormous catapult that hurled forth whole strawberry plants, with their leaves and roots, earth and gravel. Titi went on bleeding. I could hear Simon roaring with laughter. He'd laugh the other side of his face tomorrow when the gardener came to look at his strawberries. Suddenly the assault began. A missile crushed my thumb against the butt of my rifle. I sucked my hand; the nail turned quite black. Stones were raining down on us from every side. I put on my helmet. It was an outsize jam tin with a slit for the eyes, padded with cotton wool inside. My upper arms and my chest were protected by pieces of sheet-iron tied on with string. Pebbles crashed against my helmet, dented it and bruised my ears. A piece of strawberry plant got stuck in my vizor. Titi pulled it out for me. I recovered my sight and helped him to set up the machine-gun on the roof of the shed. My machine-gun consisted of a plank standing on a swivel. It had ten catapults, and a single trigger set them all firing at once . . .

Games with Titi, fights, outrageous tricks played on our farmer, the secret breeding of guinea-pigs in the landlord's Packard, which was laid up in a shed, all this was huge fun but it wasn't enough. Unconsciously I was gradually becoming the rough draft of a man, and discovering that I was all alone.

My mother was absorbed in herself. Here, too, without being able to analyse it, I felt and shared her oppression. She belonged to that tragic generation of people who are still seeking for happiness, and to whom life has not even offered the means to choose adventure.

As for my father, I never saw him. He was at Vichy all day and all night. His mind was an almost perfect piece of machinery. It did not help him to understand his wife, whom he adored, nor to grasp his own time by the forelock. Like all of us, like myself, he had been formed by a childhood which was never to let go of him.

In his mind, the spirit of freedom was constantly checked by moral preoccupations. There was the right thing to do: the way to it lay straight ahead. If you swerved to the left you drowned, if to the right you got lost.

So in my early days at Vichy I was morally deprived of parents. Deprived of love, too. Florence was no longer my governess but the person in charge of an onerous household where fifteen or twenty people were entertained to dinner every night. If she still gave me an occasional slap it was a meaningless, punitive slap. I was increasingly obsessed with sex. I felt growing within me desires that I satisfied as best a lonely child can, with dreams, with fingers.

That dream world could not be shared with Titi and his friends, nor even with my brother, who, jealous of the charm that my play-acting exercised on the grown-ups, picked quarrels with me and beat me up seven days a week, the more easily since he was two years older. It was impossible to share it with my parents, it was impossible to share anything with anybody.

About this period, then, I embarked on a double life: I took to prowling about at a time when other people were asleep. Often at two or three in the morning I would climb up on to the big, gently sloping roof and peep through the skylights into the guests' rooms, which were always occupied, and also into the maid's bedroom; she was a stout Alsatian woman of forty, and though I hated her all day long the sight of her broad rump through the curtains shocked and excited me. These stolen glimpses ranged from the bizarre to the obscene: the delightful sight of the present Director of Foreign Trade under the Chaban-Delmas Government, squeezing his nostrils in a desperate attempt to get rid of blackheads; the astonishing spectacle of a certain princess greedily kissing the private parts of a young Embassy attaché; the Dantesque vision of the maid bestraddled by our chauffeur-bodyguard, a tough workman who was a ruthless womaniser, and whose left hand, outspread against her thigh, I shall never forget—his fingers had been crushed and flattened by a machine tool. And even today after twenty years of latent insomnia, of anxious wakefulness, when sometimes, instead of sleeping, I stare as though through plate-glass at prostitutes harnessed like horses whipping haggard managing directors, when I listen eagerly to one of my girl cousins telling the detailed story of her failed suicide, when I drive while drunk, when I try to write, when I make love, I am still in quest of whatever it was I sought twenty-five years ago. The same thing that Paul Morand sought, who, aged eighty-four, told me recently with all the misery of the world in the depths of his Mongol eyes: 'I don't want to die without understanding.' Understanding what? Grasping what? Touching what?

◆

I must make a reservation. Nothing that I say has been invented, and yet as regards the exact dates and the chronology of my story, I may make mistakes. My memory is a photographer's, not an historian's, and if so-and-so claims to have left Vichy by January 1943 and by then to have been in London or Algiers for the past six months, it's quite possible that so-and-so may be right. On the other hand as regards names, faces, incidents, women's dress, men's fads, everything connected with gestures and words, sensations, emotions, the flavour of life, I don't make mistakes. I never make mistakes, or if I do it's on purpose.

Finally, my story is A-political, with a capital privative A. I have always tried to understand, and since I've never succeeded I keep on trying. As a very small boy, when I first came to Vichy in 1942, I tried to find out not what people were thinking—they never thought much and just submitted, resiliently, to events which were beyond their understanding—but rather what was happening. I listened to the radio. We got two stations, chiefly. The first bellowed: 'London will be destroyed, like Carthage.' The second, interrupted by wailings like those of a mad cat, threatened relentlessly: 'Collaborators, you'll all be shot.' In my utter bewilderment I went to ask Mother to explain. She told me: 'Darling, for the time being Vichy is the political capital of France. Frenchmen who have refused to collaborate with Ger-

53

many have other capitals, but not in France. One is in Africa, in Algiers, the other in England, in London. In Paris, administrative power is in the hands of the Germans. At Vichy you meet Japanese, Pétinists, Lavalists, and members of the Resistance movement who are Gaullists, Giraudists or Communists. You also meet *miliciens*, German civilians, Jews who are physically indistinguishable from other Frenchmen, anti-Semites of whom the worst are Rumanians, whom you might easily mistake for Jews since they don't look French. The partisans of Marshal Pétain are Pétinists, those of Prime Minister Laval are collaborators. The supporters of Algiers are Giraudists; General de Gaulle's supporters are few and far between here. Frenchmen who join the German army out of hatred for Communism are Germanophiles. Those who join the *milice* are torturers. Those who blow up trains are partisans. And those who live in big cities go hungry, irrespective of their opinions. As to where these people live, it's something like this: black marketeers live all over the place, active resisters live nowhere in particular, saboteurs live in the maquis, and people who do nothing at all live at home.'

I confess that at the time I was hopelessly confused by this explanation, about which there was nothing explicit but its lack of clarity. And yet if one is to believe such eminent works as Robert Aron's *Histoire de Vichy*, my mother was right. It's hardly reassuring for the history of France.

◆

To get into Vichy itself one had to give the countersign, and display the tricolor cockade on the windscreen of one's car. The Government, which must certainly have felt provisional, like any other government, was installed in the Hôtel du Parc, opposite the thermal springs. In front of the entrance two splendiferous soldiers stood on guard with fixed bayonets.

We took the lift that day, Mother and I. It was a huge glass cage. The attendant wore a chauffeur's cap. We got off on the second floor, and took the corridor on the left. At the corner was the door of Prime Minister Laval's office. The first person we met was Monsieur Moysset. He was an Auvergnat, a friend of the Marshal's, a former teacher at the École de Guerre. He had white hair and very black eyebrows. He kept laughing all the time, and patted my head as he explained to my mother that he was finishing a book about Proudhon. After gesticulating a bit he disappeared through a door from which there now emerged Charles Rochat, Henri du Moulin de la Barthète and Admiral Jean-Pierre Estéva.

Charles Rochat was the permanent Head of the Foreign Ministry. He was having trouble with a young member of his secretariat, who was determined to marry an English girl.

Henri du Moulin de la Barthète was the Marshal's Principal Private Secretary. He had a turned-up nose, sparse hair and a prickly temperament. This acrimonious country gentleman was later to write the only lively book on the history of Vichy: *Le Temps des Illusions*. Apparently it's full of mistakes and inventions. But does that really matter?

Admiral Estéva was the French resident Minister in Tunisia. He was a choleric old man of mystical tendencies. He used to get up at three in the morning and every time he caught hold of me he would explain: 'My boy, the tiresome thing about five o'clock mass is that it breaks up the morning.'

Mother and I made our way through this strange melting-pot in which commingled the future historian, the future Gaullist minister, and the man who was to face the firing-squad. We bumped into Monsieur Georges Bidault.* He was sober, and his future wife Suzy was with him. Then came Jean Bichelonne, Secretary of State for Industrial Production, top student of the École Polytechnique. He knew everything, and everything by heart, the Gospels, the Koran, the telephone directory. Yes, he was learning the *Bottin* by heart so as not to have to consult it. So far he had reached page 871. When he came to our house he was besieged with questions:

* Resistance leader, subsequently Foreign Minister and Prime Minister of the Fourth Republic, later exiled for plotting against the Fifth.

'What's the capital of Honduras?'

'Tegucigalpa.'

'Who wrote: "Children in the Parc Monceau play without taking off their gloves"?'

'Nobody. It was a remark made by Léon-Paul Fargue on the *terrasse* of the Café de Flore in September 1932.'

He never got anything wrong. He inflicted a crushing snub on Laval, who informed him in consternation that the Germans wanted to knock down the Eiffel Tower so as to make use of the iron.

'Tell them it doesn't weigh very much.'

'Really? How much?'

'Nine hundred thousand and twenty-seven kilograms.'

Jacques Benoist-Méchin was just leaving my father's office. He had been the chief negotiator, with Otto Abetz, of Franco-German *rapprochement*. This day-dreamer, in spite of having written a history of the German army, persisted in seeing the Third Reich as the country of Goethe and Mozart. Germany was to remain for him, as for Giraudoux, 'a demoniacal and poetic conspiracy' from which, out of the worst, a miracle might emerge. This illusion eventually brought him to the High Court, where he was to be judged in May 1947.

I had not seen him since 1942 when, in January 1969, hoping to raise the necessary cash to make a film out of his extraordinary book on Ibn Saoud, I rang him up and asked for an appointment. He then invited me to visit him at the family hunting-lodge where he was living in retirement. I had already imagined myself somewhere in the depths of Sologne when he gave me the address: the Pigalle district!

After various wanderings I eventually found the house. It was pure eighteenth century, exquisite, flanked by two shoe shops, a Bally and a Bata, the ground floor occupied by the Co-op, and an unspoilt view over a Uniprix and a Nicolas' wine-store.

If I had any sense I would describe my interview that day with that controversial figure, that eminent historian, that ailing old man. But I shan't. What I remember, and I hope he'll forgive me if he ever reads this book, is not the man himself but his hunting-lodge, deprived of its purpose, crushed by functional progress in its most hideous aspects, the revenge of Neon lighting on the age of Louis XV.

By dint of patience my mother and I eventually got into Father's office. Paul Marion, Minister of Information, was there; he was my friend, my real friend, in spite of some forty years' difference in age. He immediately grabbed hold of me and pointed out that the office, which was merely a hotel bedroom rearranged for the purpose, communicated with the next room through the back of the cupboard.

'Old man, that's the way the adulterer got out, between two piles of handkerchiefs and a row of underpants.'

He was not ribald. He was affectionate and obscene. He smiled at me, disclosing fangs stained yellow with nicotine. He frightened me. I enjoyed that. Those smiles made me feel I was sharing in something.

Paul Marion was a fanatical collaborator. Actually, he was fanatical in every field. Often when he came to see us at Charmeil we would go off alone together. He wanted me eventually, if future disasters spared me, to become a really free person. He warned me against marriage as a source of excruciating worries, and spoke in praise of free love and particularly of prostitution, extolling the fascination of promiscuous women; sex with these seemed to him an enriching, renovating experience. He detested respectable bourgeois women; he doted on creatures whom he imagined forever sprawling on silk divans, painting their toenails. His peculiar, gluttonous nature inclined him towards lyrical pornography rather than towards eroticism. He talked to me as an equal; I loved him as I loved all those who were able, and were crazy enough, to lift me out of childhood.

He died after the war, horribly painfully, of a generalized cancer. Hell had caught him alive.

My visit to Vichy that day ended with a lunch at the Chante Clair, the restaurant of the Hôtel Majestic, connected with the Hôtel du Parc by a green and yellow awning. In the 1900-style dining-room I beheld the members of the Government grouped at small tables. On my right was M. Baudoin, former Minister of Foreign Affairs, with his tiny Indochinese wife. On my left General Weygand, gaunt and still, with his Aztec's head. Straight in front Abel Bonnard, Minister of National Education. Paul Marion leaned over and said to me:

'The Marshal calls that old queen La Gestapette.'

Further on were Fernand de Brinon, Secretary of State, Jacques Leroy-Ladurie, Minister of Supply, Lucien Romier, Minister of State, Pierre Cathala, Minister of Finance, and Governor-General Brévié, Secretary of State for the Colonies.

There were more than thirty of them there, and they did not look happy. They had all gambled on Germany winning the war, on Europe being Germanized and on the need to collaborate so as to save France from the fate of Poland. Pierre Laval was deeply involved in a game of poker as risky as that which de Gaulle was playing in London. For the Germans trusted Laval as little as the British trusted de Gaulle. Both men, obliged to play an onlooker's role and forcibly prevented from influencing events, were anxiously watching the fortunes of war.

Pierre Laval's position proved untenable. One cannot govern between the hammer and the anvil. Particularly since from 1942 onwards Churchill started promising to parachute arms and provisions to the Resistance movement. The *maquis* got their arms but no provisions. Being famished, the partisans attacked farms, and Laval instituted the militia. Frenchmen hunted down Frenchmen in occupied France. Churchill was beating Laval on his own ground by deliberately introducing conditions of civil war into the country.

At that time the Hôtel du Parc, a miniature Marienbad establishment, was the scene of a sort of tragi-comedy in which courage, cowardice, absurdity and folly were inextricably mingled. If the collaboration which was being practised there seemed indispensable for the economic survival of France, it subsequently revealed itself as historically intolerable. And yet in an occupied country, riddled with agents of the Third Reich's incredible military and police infrastructure, collaboration was common sense. Resistance was hope. In any case, Vichy lost. In politics, 'that is worse than a crime, it's a mistake'.

•

Jean Giraudoux used to visit us every weekend. He was like his own Siegfried, tall, smiling, brown-haired. He wore thick horn-rimmed glasses. He was invariably accompanied by Puck, a cream-coloured poodle. His conversations with my mother were gentle and melodious and unending. Ideas, feelings, opinions which were nothing but a series of doubts drifted around them like smoke rings, played about them like kittens. They never tired of their exploration.

One stormy afternoon my mother was sitting beside him in the drawing-room. I was at their feet on the floor, mending a catapult. To begin with I didn't listen. And then there came a point when his face flushed and his voice grew jerky. It was as if he was lost in a deep wood. So I tried to understand. He was saying that it's difficult to know how to love. And then he declared that when one knows how to, it's too late, and that in any case one never succeeds in really knowing whether one loves or not. I listened with growing anguish, a lump constricting my throat. I couldn't understand everything, but his face spoke more eloquently than his words. Outside the rain fell harder. I couldn't see his eyes behind his glasses. At one point, without knowing why, I got up and burst into tears. Then Mother and Giraudoux looked at me and asked what was the matter. I was incapable of telling them. Suddenly Giraudoux must have felt guilty. He questioned me to find out whether it was because of him that I was crying. Because of him? I gave a sort of nod. He took it for an affirmative sign and began a process of investigation, going over every remark he had made. I was dying of fear. I was like a blind man on sentry duty at the top of a tower. When he re-stated the idea that one never knew whether one loved or not, I became so violently distressed that he concluded he had found the answer.

59

'Why? Aren't you like that? You know whom you love?'

Yes, I knew, but how could I formulate it? My anguish poured from my eyes, met his, and reissued from his lips. He was acting midwife, he was delivering me.

'You have the feeling that you'll know it for a long time . . . For ever?'

Tight-lipped, I screamed 'Yes', nodding frantically like a horse tossing its head. He looked at me in astonishment. He must have thought that for ever is a very long time. I think he was moved. He told me I was lucky. He was right. That luck has never deserted me, even at my worst moments. A few years later, very early, when I was about fourteen or fifteen, I knew that I should never become a priest or a soldier, or a Communist or a rich man, that I would never belong to any of those great families with whom millions of orphans find shelter. I knew that for me the real match would have to be played out with a woman, alone together. I felt that neither science nor mathematics nor music would serve to lead me to an elementary knowledge of the world and of myself. It would have to be a woman; I only had to find her.

One morning in 1960 I was at 11 bis Rue Lord Byron in Paris, working with the director Marc Allégret at putting the finishing touches to the script of a comedy whose name I've forgotten. I was hardly living with my first wife at all and I was hopelessly in love with the actress Annie Girardot. My brother Simon, who lives in Switzerland, turned up unexpectedly and told me that the younger daughter of Professor Sauvage was downstairs in her car. I had scarcely seen her since 1941, when we had met at that kindergarten party where I had been so deplorably got up as a leek. He explained to me that she dared not come upstairs for fear of meeting Vadim and his gang, and if I would go down and say hullo it would be a kind thing to do. I had no wish to be kind, and I refused. He insisted. Reluctantly, I consented at last.

A few steps away from the building, at the corner of the Rue Balzac, in front of the cinema of that name, she was waiting in a Fiat. I opened the front left-hand door and looked at her. She was twenty-four. She was busy writing on her knees, which she kept close together and slightly twisted to one side. She was wearing shoes with scuffed heels. The second-rate cut of her clothes implied that she was broke. Her nose was straight and delicate, long rather than short; her mouth perfectly proportioned. She had a brown face and brown legs, and their darkness was not due to any summer tan; it was an Arab, gipsy, Creole brownness like spicy gingerbread. Her dark hair was drawn back and tied with a shoelace at the nape of her neck. Her whole attitude revealed a good breeding which usually irritates me. She greeted me with lowered eyes, like a genuinely shy person. She seemed modest, quite cool and yet sure of her attractiveness. Her hands were slender and perfect, with just enough of the bony structure visible not to look dollish. There was an insolence in her eyes that contradicted all the rest of her. On seeing her I experienced a feeling which was strictly speaking neither sensual nor emotional, and the thought that I must get this woman for myself swept over me fiercely, calling forth my utmost cunning. In one second I realised the whole problem, which seemed insoluble. She was married, and she lived with another man with whom she was going away for good, to the United States. I was married myself. I had a daughter, a wife who would not divorce me, no money, no film contract in prospect, and above all the woman in question scarcely knew me. I was neither her friend nor her lover. I was the worst possible thing: a vague childhood acquaintance.

Only that certainty which Giraudoux had one day forced out of the depths of me, a certainty which was really only a question asked endlessly, enabled me to undertake a war in which I have won several battles but the end of which I cannot foresee. Four years of struggle, of pursuit all over Europe, to stake my claim to her. Two more years trying to offer her a certain freedom, the right to dispose of herself in thought, word and action. And yet another two years learning, myself, to be an utterly fixed mark for her, not just her husband but her home. She has always come back to me. And yet she is volatile, variable. What makes her always come back to me in the end? The wind. That's the only right course to take: open your arms wide, wait for the wind.

Before her, I had been a traveller. I had known solitary sex, my eyes clouded with a misty veil of erotic images. Then impossible love, illusory love, passion, always ending in a precipitous fall. Then love-making as a habit, intercourse at fixed times, like meals; the traditional, unchangeable rituals and the latest novelties. I had taken blows and given them. I had known voyeurs, weepers, snifflers. She suddenly freed me from all this false knowledge, as though a curtain were torn down. Light flooded in. With her I stopped lying, as all men do when they look at a woman, before even opening their lips. Before she came, I used to wander about at night to make love at random. Now I wander for the sake of dreams and discoveries, and it's such a luxury! But I don't want to assume a virtue which does not belong to me. Being a born spectator, I like to see her liked. The way she can force other people to love her I find overwhelming; as Henry Miller has said, if I were ever to think that men existed who were impervious to her charm, I would deliberately help her to ensnare them.

I was to see Jean Giraudoux regularly until the time came when he took the plane for Lisbon, one of the only towns in Europe from which he could telephone his son Jean-Pierre who, unlike his father, had chosen London.

My last memory of him goes back to the autumn of 1943. *Sodome et Gomorrhe* was then being rehearsed at the Théâtre Hébertot in Paris. At this time, the problems of telephonic communication in France were well-nigh insoluble. To speak to Edwige Feuillère, his leading lady, Giraudoux was obliged to use the direct line between our house at Charmeil and the seat of government at Vichy. From there he was put through to the Prime Minister's residence in Paris, which in turn connected him with the theatre.

Giraudoux's telephone calls took place after dinner in my

parents' bedroom, which was next to mine. I could hear every-thing. I learned that Giraudoux had a sort of rival named Claudel who was putting on a play at the same time as his: *Le Soulier de Satin*. But both of them were threatened by a third writer, Henry de Montherlant, whose play *La Reine Morte* was shortly to have its first performance. There was a war going on between poets, too.

In frozen, famished Paris, which lived under the permanent and omnipresent oppression of the Gestapo and the militia, in a Paris where tuberculosis had increased by thirty per cent since 1939, where the cost of living had gone up by a hundred and sixty-six per cent in four years, and where the death rate had risen from twelve per thousand in 1937 to eighteen per thousand, where one could not subsist for more than six days in the month on one's legal rations, where twelve torture chambers were known to be functioning twenty-four hours per day, an unprecedented blossoming of artistic creation was taking place. As in the Italian Renaissance, masterpieces sprang from a soil of blood and terror.

The season 1943-4 was among the richest ever known in Paris. The French cinema gave us *Les Enfants du Paradis*, *Les Dames du Bois de Boulogne*; in the theatre, besides Claudel, Giraudoux and Montherlant, Anouilh had just finished *Antigone*, Jean-Paul Sartre's *Les Mouches* was being played at the Théâtre de la Cité. Simone de Beauvoir published *L'Invitée*; Brasillach and Drieu were to die, but Camus and Vailland were about to emerge. What a rich harvest ...

•

This morning, in the orchard behind the house, I found a huge man, as handsome as a Greek god. He was sleeping naked under an apple tree. The early spring sunshine was gilding his skin. It was the economist Bertrand de Jouvenel, future author of that citadel nine hundred pages long, *Du Pouvoir*. At the present time he was still something of a playboy, and since his mother was Jewish he had certain worries. He was a day-dreamer, incurably lost in the mazes of his thought. I followed him about for a fortnight, fastening his shoe-laces for him, and retrieving with a butterfly net the Dunhill pipes which he left floating in the bath. From the first minute we became friends. The sort of friends you can be in wartime: all differences of age, all principles abolished. Nobody watched us. We fished for frogs all day long, talking about religion. He wanted to persuade me to go to confession. I refused. I felt that my faults were my only acquisition, my only wealth. I was quite willing to have them blessed, but I refused to have them taken away. My theories drew from him cries of horror which eventually scared the frogs and toads, driving them away from our favourite pond into another quieter one some fifty metres further off. We were left there, *tête à tête*, with our useless rods and red rags. He called me a schismatic and a heretic. I had no idea what that meant but it upset me. To comfort me, he offered me his whole fortune: a Swiss knife with six blades and a corkscrew. By dint of listening in on drawing-room gossip I learned that he had had a great love affair with the novelist Colette. Everybody was wondering whether or not he was the hero of a novel entitled *Chéri*. So that I finally put the question to him, during one of our fishing parties. He answered immediately and unequivocally:

'No. That wasn't me, it was the other fellow.'

'Which other fellow?'

'The one who wore suede shoes. I was the one who took pot shots at the Colonne Vendôme from the windows of the Ritz, with a gun made of a curtain rod stuffed with buckshot.'

Since the one remaining frog which had not left the pond bit at that moment, and since Bertrand de Jouvenel left the house that night, I never learned the sequel. Several times, after the war, I wanted to ask him for it. But he was not so young by then, and I was older. Nothing was the same any more.

◆

Stanislas, Vicomte de la Rochefoucauld, was a huge ungainly

creature. An affable melancholy lurked in the depths of his shrewd eyes. He had a habit of laughing noiselessly, opening an enormous mouth. This sporadic gaiety seemed like a perpetual polite sob. One day he took the Jardin family to spend the weekend not far from Vichy, with his uncle, the old Comte de Bourbon-Busset.

Thirty kilometres from Lapalisse stood the feudal castle of the Bourbons with its panoply of high battlemented towers, aggressively machicolated. When Mother and I saw the drawbridge being lowered we gave a shudder. Stanislas completed our demoralization by breaking it to us that we weren't going to have much fun, as his Busset cousins, ever since leaving the Court in the reign of Louis XI, had remained very military-minded.

And so it turned out. M. de Bourbon-Busset, who had recently lost a son, received us like the commander of a citadel. He took us slowly round various strategic works, redoubts, walls, posterns, barbicans, bartizans, which in their time had discouraged the Dukes of Burgundy from seizing Auvergne but had proved powerless to keep back the Germans. Then he made me shoulder the hunting rifle used by Louis XV as a child, and admire the sword of his ancestor François-Louis-Antoine, who had covered himself with glory at the siege of Hanover in 1757.

The skilly we were served at dinner in the guardroom, waited on by a squint-eyed servant with a limp, under the metallic glare of some thirty suits of armour, completed my depression.

I had plenty of nightmares that night, sleeping in a seventeenth-century bed between tapestry curtains depicting devils and unicorns. At ten next morning I was woken by my father, dressed in a dark suit, and my mother in a huge grey felt hat. Through winding passages we reached the chapel. To my surprise we were in a box overlooking the high altar and all the main body of the building. Some nine yards below, peasants and villagers were attending Mass. I was pushed on to a satin *prie-Dieu*. On my right was Marshal Pétain in civilian dress, and his wife in a flowered frock that made her look like a gigantic peony.

The harmonium played Bach. Swallows flew in through a

broken window. Terrified by the incense and the music, they swooped about the nave.

As we went out Maman was filmed by a cameraman from *Actualités françaises*. Papa called out: 'Stand straight, Simone.'

But she noticed nothing and went on picking flowers in the moat, which was overgrown with weeds. My father looked happy. He often did when he looked at my mother. Never when he spoke to her. What has become of my mother as she then was? I want to talk about her, but I can't. When I started this book I thought my mother would be its king-pin, that the whole story would revolve around her radiant presence. Why am I thus mute about her, why does my father appear as a widower throughout these pages? What has happened to the woman whom I called Simone, like any friend of hers? Not like any friend, like her best friend. I was her closest and most intimate friend. I am sadly afraid now that I'm no more than her son. And yet there was never any quarrel between us, never a word to suggest the slightest estrangement. So what has happened? Nothing tangible, only that the state of utter transparency that had lasted over a quarter of a century had one day become clouded and opaque. Our affection remained, but the spirit had gone out of it. About 1965 she stopped looking at me and began to look at herself, while I stopped looking at her and looked at my wife. She was seeing ahead to her own death, while I, at last, was embarking on my real life. There was a mute and tragic divorce which both of us always refused to acknowledge. This is why I am unable to give any account of the woman that she was. And yet she was superb, physically and morally. Her nonconformity was breathtaking; she would pass from reticence to the liveliest provocativeness. She was afraid of nothing, and this daring, combined with her beauty, engendered an ever-fresh youthful vitality which, it seemed, nothing would ever check. For nearly thirty years I knew what she was thinking even before she thought it. Now, I no longer know what's going on within her. Thinking has banished her gaiety, her passion for understanding everything prevents her from taking action, even with regard to the most

66

elementary domestic matters. She irritates me. I love her, but I resent her acceptance of old age. I love her wrinkles but not the way she has come to a full stop. Previously she had seemed ageless, and within herself was one of the freest human beings one could ever hope to meet. Today I sometimes wonder if she hasn't forgotten part of her life. Is that necessary in order to survive, once old age has entered into us? At what point does one become old? Sickness, fear, despair, things which hitherto have only brushed us with a casual wing—at what point do we feel them in the heart's core, and give up the struggle for ever? And at what point must we brutally reject those we have adored in order to stay alive ourselves? I don't know when, I only know that I did that to my mother.

♦

I found it hard to understand exactly what being a Jew meant. I could see no difference between my own appearance and the appearance of the Jews I met every day. If at least Jews had had red or black skins the Germans would be killing people who were unlike themselves. As it was, they were murdering other Germans because they were Jews. So it was not a question of nationality, since Jews could be French or Italian or Hungarian.

I was baffled by something incomprehensible. It was so arbitrary that it upset even a child like myself. I was frightened, frightened for my own sake and for my family's. What was there to prove that tomorrow the Germans would not decree that all children with brown hair or all blue-eyed women must be killed? Criminals are condemned for murder, but Jews were being exterminated even when they were children and had done nothing at all.

All the questions I put to Dr. Robert Worms, who had now come to stay in the room next to mine, received answers which were themselves fresh questions. I soon had to accept the shocking fact that he himself did not know why the Jews were being killed! I could not quite believe in his total sincerity. I would rather he had been guilty; that would have reassured me.

'But what have you done to the Germans?'

'Nothing.'

'Then why do they want to kill you?'

'For no reason.'

'But there must be a reason?'

'I am a Jew.'

'How can one recognize a Jew?'

'They say you can tell by his nose.'

'People aren't killed because of their noses?'

'Yes, millions of people.'

'But why?'

'I don't know.'

He smiled, stroked my hair and began to sing again.

♦

Splendid weather; torrid heat. There was an atmosphere of nervous tension. Our friends who were pro-Algiers flew off every day in semi-secrecy from the tiny aerodrome of Charmeil, below our house on the banks of the Allier. The grown-ups, convinced that something dreadful would inevitably happen and that most of them would die, had stopped guarding their speech in front of the child that I was. All these men who clung to their ideas like dogs to a bone fascinated me. Later, when peace broke out, restoring them all to their everyday preoccupations, I was to be cruelly disillusioned.

Baron Pierre Ordioni arrived from Algiers with a sun-dazed head and a suitcase containing his Spahi captain's uniform, packets of dates and three gigantic grasshoppers. I was profoundly impressed by this desperado, a cousin of the Pozzo di Borgos, former *aide de camp* to Marshal Lyautey, with his limp, his monocle, and his whirling cane. After lunch I went to see him in the bedroom where he was having his siesta. I found him lying naked, hairy as an ape, snoring like a dragon. He woke up when I came in and scratched his groin.

68

'Old man, nothing's to be taken seriously except love and war, which must be taken tragically.'

He was mystical, violent, unjust and tender-hearted, a man of the Middle Ages although his title dated from the Second Empire. After dinner, when we were going into the drawing-room, he heard me call my brother Simon a bloody fool. His eyeglass fell out, he grabbed my arm and squeezed it ferociously:

'Do you know, you rascal, that one day my father heard me call my sister a cow and gave me a thrashing.'

I protested. Then he called me a sissy and a drip, declaring that violence is the salt of life and that in his youth, a time which then seemed to me as remote as that of the Gauls, men were brought up as men. Since assertions of principle have always puzzled me, I asked him how I had been brought up.

'You've not been brought up at all, that's your great attraction.'

Throughout the rest of the evening he talked to me about a stupendous notion which had never entered my head, the notion of suicide. The supreme choice, which consists in deciding for oneself the day and the hour of one's death. I was haunted by this idea for several days. I revelled in it. Ordioni had pointed out that it is an exclusively human privilege; that apart from the scorpion and the whale, animals never destroy themselves. The film *The Battle*, which I had seen recently and in which Sessue Haya Kawa thrusts a sword into his own bowels, finally convinced me that to be really adventurous one ought to take the leap deliberately, of one's own free will, instead of waiting for war or sickness to carry one off unprepared, at the wrong moment, without consulting one as to the day or the month. After a night of frenzied reflection, my mind was made up. The very next morning I prepared methodically for a kind of hara-kiri which I hoped would be painless.

Alone in the coal-cellar, sitting cross-legged, by the light of a candle I set to work, hammering a nail into the end of a huge cartridge from a naval machine gun, pinched from a friend whose father was an officer in the Navy. After every blow struck on the detonator of the cartridge case, I was surprised to find myself still alive. Unwittingly reproducing Pascal's wager about the hereafter, I mumbled a few *Our Fathers* so that, if God existed, I should still have some chance of going to heaven. One particularly violent blow made the missile explode, with a terrific noise. Part of the huge pile of coal came crashing down on me. My head hit the ground violently. My eyes were wide open and yet I could see nothing. After a moment's thought I concluded I must be dead. I waited expectantly for angels or devils or something: nobody came. Yes, voices! My brother's and that of my friend Titi, the carpenter's son.

'Let's see if he's done for,' my brother said.

He grabbed hold of my nose and twisted it ferociously. I was howling wildly: 'Help, I'm blind.'

'No, you goof, it's just that the draught's blown out the candle.'

The day after this failed suicide, my friend Ordioni, an ardent anti-Vichyist, left to go back to North Africa. His farewells were passionate. He kissed each member of the family a dozen times, leapt on to a bicycle and made his way secretly to the airfield. Ten minutes later his twin-engined plane flew over the house. I could see him looking out through the porthole, smiling at me. Would I ever see him again? Some people said he'd be killed in North Africa. But others said it was those who stayed in Vichy who would be killed . . .

◆

The more troubled the times became, the fuller our life seemed to be. The house was never empty by day or by night. On 22nd June, Laval's speech declaring that he hoped for a German victory struck all France with dismay. Even at Vichy, among collaborators, there were arguments and attempts at interpretations. Some people wanted to leave the ship before it sank; some wanted to kill Laval; for others, he was the man who would save them from the worst. Around me, conversations and debates were raging. About midnight, exhausted by the buzzing in this demented beehive, longing for a little sleep, I took my pillow and my eiderdown into a tent that had been pitched behind the house, in the middle of the lawn. But even here the voices of night walkers pursued me. I recognized those of my father and Jacques Bousquet. I stuck my head out of my shelter to look at them.

'Don't stay there,' Bousquet told me, 'you'll get kidnapped.'

He was a very handsome man of thirty-five. Born in Languedoc, he had been thrust very early into political life by Albert Sarraut, who made him a prefect at the age of twenty-nine. For the time being, he was Director-General of Police; the Germans were to deport him in 1944.

Absorbed in their mad political dreams, the two men soon forgot me. Without moving a single yard away, they went on talking just above my head, scattering cigarette ash on me. Bousquet declared that Laval's latest speech had thoroughly discredited him. As my father did not reply, Bousquet said: 'Didn't you speak to him about that?' The half-smoked cigarette wobbled on my father's lip as he answered:

'Yes, I told him: "If the Allies win the war, you'll be hanged . . ." '

'And then?'

'He replied: "And that's not a bad end for a politician." '

The machinery had started up, and it was going to crush everything. By the end of June 1942 the Jews were being hunted down everywhere. Acts of violence against the Germans were now not confined to the occupied zone. They took place in the 'free' zone too. German police came into Vichy itself to arrest Frenchmen. There was nobody in front of the Hôtel du Parc where, a year and a half before, the Marshal had been greeted with cheers. Armed groups of soldiers stood on guard day and night. The real power of the Government was crumbling away daily. German prisoners interned in the Southern zone for spying were forcibly released by the Gestapo. On 14th July 1942, in the very heart of Vichy, five hundred people answered the call of the dissident de Gaulle and, for the first time, demonstrated against the collaborating Government.

Meanwhile, life went on, frantically. That evening, my room was occupied by Jacques Leroy-Ladurie, Minister of Food, a giant with a stentorian voice. He vociferated, accusing the German authorities of disregarding their agreements and laying hands on the scanty supplies still left him to feed the French. But Jacques Barnaud, delegate-general for Franco-German relations, to whom his complaints were addressed, declared he could do nothing about it.

My father, meanwhile, was shut up in his room with Paul Marion and Joseph Barthélemy, Minister of Justice.

In the only bathroom of our house, Maurice Martin du Gard, sitting on the edge of the bath-tub, was telling my mother—who didn't seem at all interested—why the Munich conference had been bound to lead to war.

In a visitors' room Jacques Baraduc, a young lawyer, disciple of the illustrious Leon Bérard, was playing chess with his invalid mother. This young Auvergnat, very handsome in a sinister way, was later to be one of Pierre Laval's defending counsel.

Down below, in the enormous drawing-room, Yvonne Printemps, paying a brief visit with Pierre Fresnay, sang her latest hit: Alain Gerbault's medley. Jacques Février accompanied her on the piano. When she had finished she jumped on to the billiard table and did the splits on the green baize.

His Excellency Lequerica, Spanish Ambassador to Vichy, a gigantic golden turkey-cock, pot-bellied like one of Charles V's galleons, was nearly swooning with delight.

Close by, in a sometime dressing-room converted into a bedroom, a marvellous country doctor, Jean Giraudoux's brother, administered resounding smacks to our new little Norman maid. The girl, who helped our fat monster of an Alsatian cook, was the daughter of an alcoholic, given to sleep-walking and a sufferer from anorexia nervosa among other ills; she was deliberately dying of hunger. Only a hearty spanking from Dr. Giraudoux could impel her to take nourishment. He saved her life.

•

Paul Morand came hurtling into my life. He was to remain forever part of it. One sunny morning about nine o'clock I saw a cyclist climbing up the path towards our house. He was pedalling as energetically as a character in a silent film. When he reached the steps the man, who looked like a sort of Tartar, flung down his bicycle and climbed through the open window into the drawing-room. He was swaying like a drunken sailor. Fifty years' horseback riding had made dry land seem like the deck of a trawler. He kissed my mother, who was having her breakfast, seized my cup of ersatz chocolate, drank it off, made a face, pointed to me as though I were some object and asked whether I could swim. The answer being negative, he bundled me on to his carrier, bicycled down to Vichy and threw me into the swimming-pool at the Tennis Club. I was rescued just in time by Countess Jean de Beaumont, a superb stalwart blonde. 'Call me Paule', she told me, thumping me on the back. I hadn't time; barely time to spit out the chlorinated water that was choking me.

We set off again forthwith to the banks of the Allier . . . Here we went boating and water-cycling. We rowed like galley-slaves. We landed on marshy islands where young nudist couples were hiding. We drank grenadine in open-air waterside cafés and listened to records of Léo Marjane. Morand was constantly on the go. He maintained absolute silence. After a week of this frenzied way of life I asked him to talk to me a little. 'Impossible,' he replied, 'I'm all tied up inside.' Like the hero of his novel *L'Homme pressé* (The Man in a Hurry), Morand was prey to a feverishness which owed nothing to the outside world. He was born in a hurry, and he will die in a hurry. He is possessed by what Saint-Exupéry calls 'a nostalgia for elsewhere'. Convinced that real life is going on beyond the skyline, he spends his life trying to catch up with it. When he keeps still, however much he tries to live in the moment that moment eludes him and slips away between his fingers. I have seen him push his way between customers at the bar of the Hôtel Plazza and hustle the barman to get served faster, and then contemplate his whisky regretfully.

73

He'd been given it too late, he was no longer thirsty. Had he really been thirsty at all, that day?

In 1930 he tore through Europe in a monstrous red Bugatti Royale, like some strange apocalyptic fireman hurrying to put out the fires of hell. Where was he going? Although he had been all round the world ten times at least he can never have gone to any place, since as soon as he got anywhere he was gone again. Today, aged over eighty, he still scorches along at the wheel of a Porsche 911. He will drive non-stop from Paris to Madrid to stare intently for a few moments at a Velazquez, some detail of which he has forgotten, and then leave again like the wind, without even taking a cup of coffee.

Incredibly neurotic, introverted to the point of mental asphyxia, he has never really been able to talk. And yet he tries to, periodically. Disastrously, the words he utters don't represent his thoughts. Only in flashes can he say what he really means. These generally occur when one is engaged with him in some precise manual activity: 'The only totalitarian régime I'm really afraid of is woman's.' At such moments the door opens a crack, and I see fragments of what's inside his head. 'I don't want to die without having understood . . . My own tragedy is emptiness. I've never had an inner life. And is it true that you love your wife?'

By the time I've tried to answer him his mind is on something else, or he has left the room. He does not believe in answers, questions are enough for him.

He is a pyramid of contradictions, swivelling round; what is he really? His political career has been a triumph of clumsiness. He is just the opposite of Talleyrand. Holding a diplomatic post in London in 1939, he made the blunder of returning to Paris. Chance put him among the collaborators, and he then drew another unlucky card in 1943 when he let himself be appointed ambassador to Bucharest. He hoped to find peace in Rumania, a country of which his wife, the former Princess Soutzo, was practically part-owner. He was wrong again. A year later the Russians came in and took everything away from him. My

74

father just managed to save his life by getting him sent as ambassador to Berne, two months before the Liberation. Like Claudel, like Saint-John Perse, he never chose to be a diplomat. At the beginning of this century, upper middle-class families sent their scholarly sons to the Quai d'Orsay, just as the younger sons of eighteenth-century aristocrats were put into the Church. For Morand's generation diplomacy was neither a profession nor an art, but a career. It opened the way for advantageous international marriages and enabled one to cross frontiers with British-made suitcases full of chocolate and sealed with sealing-wax.

What is it that's so special about this unstable, uncertain man? To begin with, he was Proust's friend. And then, as a writer, he was one of the chief inventors of our present-day style. When Morand's writing first appeared in France it owed nothing to anybody, it was as new as jazz, as precise as photography. Roger Nimier, Antoine Blondin, François Nourissier, Jacques Laurent and to some extent Sagan have learnt from it, whether consciously or not. Morand founded a school, although its fame is ebbing now. But when the tide turns again, at the equinox, he'll be as conspicuous as the oil-slick left by the *Torrey Canyon*.

All the Morands that I know, from the prodigious author of *Hécate et ses chiens* to the visionary interpreter of Dostoyevsky, to the horseman, the cook, the traveller, all these characters set end to end would scarcely make up half of himself. The other part of him, his backbone, sometimes his steel corselet, the person through whom he has alternately lost and recovered his real self, is his wife. In 1970 they were still passionately in love with one another. This is very impressive. I maintain here that Morand is the only man in France, maybe in the whole world, who has given his wife a wild mink coat on her ninety-third birthday out of sheer love and delight, to make her feel beautiful.

I got to know Hélène Morand at Vichy in the summer of 1942, shortly after her husband had begun teaching me his two specialities, horse-riding and mental anguish. She is a tiny slenderly built creature, Greek by birth and with a Greek profile, though

75

with somewhat the look of an owl when seen full-face; her character is like nobody else's. The daughter of an Athenian banker, Rumanian through her first marriage and French through her second, her vast fortune and her possessions make her a citizen of all Europe. In 1942 she still had homes here and there between the Esterel and the Urals. Her culture is all-embracing; she speaks eleven languages and at the time of writing is perfecting her knowledge of Chinese for the sake of the future. Hélène Morand is probably the only woman Proust ever really loved, apart from his mother. His passion for her assumed the most secretive and seemingly negative forms. He adored Hélène's feet and forbade her to show them to other people. For the sake of peace and quiet, when she had visitors and he was present, she lay on a divan with a fur rug covering her legs.

The first time I saw her at Charmeil she looked me up and down and then said to her grandson, Prince Jean-Albert de Broglie, who had come with her:

'Just look, darling, what shocking manners young Pascal has.'

The prince, a fat moon-faced twelve-year-old, squinted at me slily and went one better:

'Yes, Granny, not good form at all, not the sort of thing one likes.'

I took my revenge that very evening by kicking the prince down the main staircase. I might even have been said to score a try, since he fell on his head and tore his 'Old England' suit.

The incident caused some sensation, but had an unexpected consequence: far from incurring the wrath of his illustrious grandmother, I gained her friendship. Little by little, as the days passed, she even managed to comfort me for being so badly brought-up.

She was appalled by French ways. Brought up in the subtly refined atmosphere of old European courts, she could not get used to Morand's turning up with Cocteau and Auric and shouting to her, in front of her household:

'Hurry up and get dressed, I'll take you to the bistro and we'll have a good blow-out.'

Even today she hasn't yielded an inch. She disapproves of contemporary sexual habits. Not like other old ladies, for moral reasons, but because her tired old eyes haven't noticed that fashions have changed:

'Darling, how boring for all those girls to spend their time unlacing their stays and lying down on sofas.'

When I told her that girls have stopped wearing knickers and make love standing up, she felt hopeful once again. What she dreaded most for the younger generation was the waste of time.

In that Central Europe where she spent her own youth, an exquisite art of living existed side by side with feudal savagery. In Rumania, peasants suspected of theft had their fingers cut off, refractory housemaids were handed over to the coachman to be beaten with cudgels or whips. Hélène Morand had thus witnessed more in her eighty-three years than a Frenchman could have done by living from Louis XI's time to that of Fallière. Her scale of values reflected this. She will never cease to surprise me. For her, the Russian Revolution of 1917 was just a casual incident, whereas the real catastrophe was 1914. Not because it was the beginning of a war which was to bleed France white, this *condottiere* did not care about that, but because general mobilization meant the end of large households, the disappearance of her supernumerary flunkeys into the maw of greedy battlefields. Yes, she could never forgive her retainers for having exchanged their livery for horizon-blue uniforms.

I cannot say in what year these two exceptional beings came together. All I know is that he informed her of his love one Christmas night. It was in Bucharest. Hélène, who was then married to Prince Soutzo, had organized a Christmas tree in her palace. Not for children, for whom she never cared, but for her friends. It was a live Christmas tree: herself, covered with jewels, carrying candles, garlanded with gold wreaths, standing on a Roman chariot drawn by white horses. The gifts strewn about her feet were motionless men disguised as teddy-bears, rabbits, monkeys or cats. As the chariot moved forward along an immense gallery, Hélène offered these 'toy animals' to the pretty women present, who later took them as partners for the ball. She was preparing to hand out a big Saint Bernard when the creature said to her: 'Don't give me away, keep me for yourself.' This dog was Morand. Since that day she has called him *mon gros toutou*, my big bow-wow.

Paul and Hélène Morand are incurable wanderers; they have spent their lives camping out, sometimes in embassies, sometimes in their various houses, which are always startling in size and appearance. The stronghold in the Champ de Mars which is their Paris home was designed by Hélène in 1913. It has a drawing-room 38 metres long and 9·50 metres high. This Citizen Kane dwelling was conceived on purpose to house a pair of colossal cupboards from the Imperial Palace in Peking. Nijinsky danced there; the first performance of Bourdet's *Le Sexe Faible* took place there before an audience of five hundred close friends. Half-way up the wall was a heavy grille opening on to a dark room. This was the musicians' jail, where Hélène imprisoned her band during receptions. This barbarous custom has become obsolete owing to the use of gramophone records.

At Vevey, on the edge of the lake, there stands the neo-Gothic Château de l'Aile, the Morands' Swiss retreat. It's like an outlaw's den realized by Douglas Fairbanks and restored by Viollet le Duc: it's panelled in wild cherrywood with ebony ceilings, and chandeliers more suitable for use as flying trapezes than for lighting the home.

Immediately after the Liberation, exiled and penniless, they had rented a half-ruined villa above Montreux, connected with the town by a private funicular. Later on, I visited their caravanserai at Tangier—thirty-two rooms and a leaking roof. And they have gone on living thus in a totally disorganized way ever since the war, often without any servants, in a permanent disorder like that of life itself. They never stay anywhere; they just pass through. There's always a Marie Laurencin peeping out of a half-packed suitcase, a Gobelins tapestry used as a bedspread, perfumes, tobacco, spirits, riding-boots propped up

78

against a Ferrari motor-wheel, tattered books, Persian cats and blond chows putting out their violet tongues.

•

Mid-September 1942. Once again, society had got the better of me. Once again I found myself incarcerated in a school, the village school at Charmeil. The mistress was a worthy country-woman who read *Quatre-Vingt-Treize* to us with great expression. I still couldn't read, but I duly absorbed one of the finest pieces of dialogue in the French language:
'Who are you?'
'I am a woman taking flight with her children.'
'Where do you come from?'
'I don't know . . . a battle . . .'
It was some six weeks before the mistress discovered that I could not read. My visual and auditive memory was so well trained that when one of my schoolfellows had read the lesson I could repeat it by heart, pretending to follow it in the book. I could even remember where to turn the page. Only one day when I blundered, I was called to account and sent to the bottom of the class. It was total disgrace. The teacher refused to believe that I couldn't read, since she had seen me reading. Then my troubles began. I had to have private lessons. The result was nil. I discovered later that I was dyslexic. That's to say that among other defects I suffered from nervous troubles which prevented me from understanding what I read. I was left-handed, a frus-trated left-hander, a visual left-hander, and my poor bewildered brain turned the words wrong way round and persisted in making me read from right to left instead of from left to right. Nowadays children who suffer from this defect are cured in a few weeks by a new method of mental therapy. In my day the method used was a box on the ear and a kick on the backside. This did not produce good results.

As regards arithmetic I was no more brilliant. I was, and I still am, allergic to figures. Even today the rule of three is a

79

total mystery to me. I shall die without having solved it.

Then there was geography. I hated it. I loathed those horrible lists of unknown places. How much time I have wasted irremediably, learning to locate towns and countries, whereas there are railway time-tables and perfectly efficient information services in every airport.

I can still see myself standing in front of the blackboard in my short pants, biting my nails, lost in the midst of a desert of ignorance vaster than the Sahara.

'Pascal Jardin, what is meant by the rural habitat?'

'The rural habitat is something to do with streets—*rues* . . .'

'No marks.'

And history: Louis XI used to shut cardinals up in cages . . . The Hundred Years War lasted seventy years . . . Louis XV was called The Well-Beloved but everybody hated him.

The most hopeless illiterate, the stupidest dunce, the most abysmally uneducated country bumpkin would inevitably develop more commonsense than the wretch forced to fabricate a sham culture for himself out of such pitiful elements.

My confidence sapped by my utter inability to understand conventional lessons, even more disgusted by this primary school than by the religious institution I had been sent to at Bernay, exasperated by the various establishments at which I subsequently put in brief appearances, such as Le Rosay, a Swiss boarding school for multi-millionaires, where in 1944 I had the privilege of smashing, with a well-aimed punch, the spectacles of the future king of the Belgians—Squinting Bobo to me—or the *lycée* at Evreux, in 1948, that Napoleonic barracks which was de-molished four years later, where I carried rebelliousness to the point of pissing against the blackboard—it was not until after the Liberation, when I met Raymond Abellio, novelist and mathemati-cal philosopher, author of *Heureux les Pacifiques* and of *La Bible, document chiffré* (The Bible as a coded document), that I finally got down to work.

I came to know him in Switzerland in 1949. I was fifteen. It was an eye-opener. Abellio, a graduate of the École Polytech-nique and a distinguished engineer—he had built the tunnel for the Autoroute de l'Ouest—was a friend of Edith Piaf and of Simone Weil, and he was wanted by the police of the entire world. He had formerly been a Trotskyist, then an extreme right-wing militant, collaborating with the *cagoulard* Deloncle; he was hiding in a small village called Chexbres above Lausanne. My parents, at their wits' end, handed me over to him. For three years he tried to educate me, to make me an *honnête homme*, a well-bred man in the eighteenth-century sense. He taught me fencing, since I used to slouch about with my stomach out, he supervised my first love affair with a 'mature woman', made me read Retz and Saint-Simon so that even if I couldn't spell I should appreciate the music of the French language. He re-read for me and with me St. Augustine, Pascal, Descartes, Shakespeare and Sartre. And he made me study history haphazardly, jumping from the Punic wars to the wars of religion, explaining the rudiments of the origins of Socialism by readings that moved backwards from Jaurès to Marx, completing the whole by stories of the Spanish war, in which Catalonia appeared as a sort of Promised Land, a potential anarchist state during the period of its break with orthodox Communism. Anarchism, in his view, meant order, and at the level at which he understood the term there could be no possible confusion in my mind between his spiritual quest and what is commonly meant by disorder. His black flag was not flown in the street but somewhere deep down at the confines between knowledge and madness.

◆

September 1942. In front of the Hôtel du Parc, close to the thermal establishment, chairs were set out in a row. All the members of the Laval government were there, as well as the diplomatic corps. Monsieur Monoto, the Japanese ambassador, presented a particularly high-class exhibition of judo. Mother was wearing a garden-party hat by Jeanne Lanvin and incredible sandals of plaited blue paper from Hermes. On the square arena, a sort of open boxing-ring, white-clad samurai made fierce animal noises as they crushed one another's necks and trampled on each other's stomachs. All the yellow men present looked on unflinchingly; the Europeans seemed dumbfounded. Marshal Pétain was nodding sadly. What can a soldier be thinking about when he's neither a dreamer nor a writer, when he's not Caesar nor even de Gaulle? About nothing, perhaps.

. . . On my left was the régime's professional intellectual, Bichelonne, Secretary of State for industrial production. He was talking to my father, who for lack of a Lucky Strike was puffing at a Balto. Things seemed to be going badly. Apparently the Marshal's National Revolution was openly at odds with the muscular Republic that Laval was aiming at . . . And everything was in a muddle, and the war would go on, and my mother was angelically beautiful, and the Japs were fighting one another like Chinese dragons, and people were being killed in the camps, and America was arming, and the world seemed about to fall apart, and forty million were going to die; and yet thirty years later nothing has changed except for the names. Jews have become Palestinians, helpless minorities are still suffering just as much and new genocides are looming.

That summer afternoon in 1942 drew gently to its close. The sun was setting. It must have been seven o'clock, nearly supper time. I followed my mother through the streets of Vichy, that ephemeral capital, that blunder in a badly mismanaged period of French history. How lovely the sunset was over the Allier, where Danielle Darrieux and Rubirosa were belatedly canoeing together; how sweet that wartime sunset was, how gentle in a time of terror. My memory unendingly recalls that desperate summer when France, raped like a girl, was groping for a way out. The idea of liberty is a funny thing; it dies like a cut flower as soon as you grasp it.

◆

Autumn 1942. In my father's car, driving back from Vichy to Charmeil, was a tiny scrap of a woman; *Couchés dans le foin, Quand un vicomte . . ., C'est un jardinier qui boite*: Mireille.

Mireille, who would have liked to be six foot tall and to play Phèdre, Mireille who was a Jewess in flight from the Gestapo. She was accompanied by her husband, Emmanuel Berl. This extraordinary creature, whose physical presence seemed constantly swamped by his over-active intellectual life, already, at this period, looked like a musk-rat, like a comical ghost haunting the Palais-Royal, where he had been living for a long time and where he still lives. A former editor of the left-wing weekly *Marianne*, a friend of Colette's and of Cocteau's, he had broken off relations with Drieu la Rochelle because of the latter's Germanophilia and then with Malraux whose unqualified Gaullism had begun to irritate him. His thirst for freedom could not tolerate any partisanship.

I sat in front, beside Father who was at the wheel. I could see Emmanuel Berl in the driving-mirror. He looked like Moses making Marx-Brother faces. He played with ideas as one plays with a ball, and with words as one bowls a hoop. He drove them in front of him, hoping they would keep going as long as possible without collapsing.

He was afraid of being caught, afraid of an atrocious slow death, and yet his sense of humour remained unaffected. Perhaps because he had already seen that very death at close quarters. In 1915, in the front line, he had been buried alive by a shell; in the pocket of his tunic there was a hundred-page letter from Proust on the subject of jealousy. When they finally dug him up the letter had gone, and so had part of his stomach.

For the time being, he was listening to my father telling him that the Vichy Government had just decided to shut down a boarding school kept by a couple of academics, Jean-Paul Sartre and Simone de Beauvoir. They let their boy and girl pupils sleep together at nights. Some parents had got wind of the thing and there had been a scandal. Berl slowly wrinkled that quivering radar scanner, his nose. After a moral and physical sniff, he concluded:

'Surely it's in the nature of things that boys should go with girls . . . Unless your government would rather the boys slept together and the girls did likewise?'

One can argue with anybody, but not with one's chromosomes. Today, at thirty-six, I am no longer strictly speaking my father's son but rather a replica of himself. To begin with, we have the same gestures, the fag-end clinging to the lips so that smoke gets into one's left eye. And then we have the same way of inveigling and seducing other people. He has bequeathed me his incurable pessimism, disguised as frantic high spirits.

Who is Jean Jardin, who is my father? That's a question I often ask myself. So do other people. He made me, willy-nilly. Even though I reject his religious, political and moral beliefs *en bloc*, even so, even today, even at a distance, the weight of his hand makes me bow my back.

We have an account to settle, he and I. Is it between the two of us? For a long time I believed it was. When I was fifteen, one evening when he wanted to stop me from going to the cinema (he never went, and I already went every day), after a violent confrontation, I pushed him down the stairs. He might have broken his neck but, supple as a cat, he caught hold of the banisters.

No, I realize now that the account we have to settle is not between ourselves. Mine is with life, his is with society.

The son of a Bernay shopkeeper, brought up in the shadow of the estate managers of the Ducs de Broglie, he decided one day that he was going to get into the château, into all other châteaux. His excessively humble childhood gave him a kind of superstitious terror of poverty. He avoids bistros and second-class hotels, he likes only enormous, reassuring luxury establishments. Certain objects, such as sewing-machines which directly remind him of his childhood, are strictly banished from the houses he lives in. Since he cannot endure the people around him having financial worries, and Heaven knows there are always plenty of such people, he'll make untold sacrifices to help them out at the end of the month. Unlike most of his contemporaries, he can face his own money problems very well, but not other people's. Is it from generosity? Yes and no. It's rather from a desire to assume responsibility for other people, so that they shall remain under his tyrannical sway and spell.

He is always ready to invite any friends of mine to dinner, in unlimited numbers, provided he may choose the restaurant and the menu. He uses the direct method.

'Obviously nobody here is going to be stupid enough to ask for steak! So it'll be caviar and sweetbreads for everyone.'

On one occasion a newcomer, a stockbroker, tactless fellow, said foolishly: 'I don't like sweetbreads.'

'Well, you're going to like these, they're being cooked specially for me!'

In 1914, at the age of ten, when he was a boarder at the Evreux *lycée*, he suffered a terrible attack of decalcification, which his family made no attempt to have cured. Thus, long before he was full grown, his spine was irremediably twisted, depriving him of some ten centimetres of his proper height and condemning him to incessant pain for life. He grew up a misogynist, a passionate, unjust man, highly cultured, liable to unforeseeable fits of violence; his great eyes seemed too large for his tormented face, eyes like those of Anouilh's *La Sauvage*, who cannot sleep as long as a lost dog is howling somewhere in the world. He was a desperately hard worker, toiling like any nineteenth-century proletarian; between the ages of twenty-four and fifty he spent seventy hours a week in his office; he never took a real holiday until he was sixty. A tough sick man, sleeping three hours a night, at death's door by four in the afternoon and then galvanized into life by six, racked at dawn by ferocious bouts of coughing due to his consumption of three packets of Gitanes a day, swallowing coffee by the litre and treating his perpetual neuralgia with dry champagne, this frail dynamo was subject to painful skin eruptions that affected his eyelids. As a small child I used to hear him nicknamed Le Borgne, 'one-eye', when he concealed his affliction behind dark glasses with leather flaps at the side to keep out the cold air.

And yet in 1942 my father had an irresistible charm which took the place of beauty. Always dressed in exquisitely cut grey flannel suits, wearing pre-war shoes from London, he carried a flat black automatic under his left arm, and this I found most awe-inspiring.

Often in the evenings I would escape from the house about half-past eight and go along the Vichy road all by myself to meet him. It was liable to be a long and frightening journey, for nobody ventured in the darkness along the deserted roads of occupied France. And when I saw two headlights, I knew without any possibility of doubt that it was he, that I was safe. His car, a 15 h.p. Citroën with bullet-proof windows and huge wheels from Delahaye's, could do over 180 kilometres an hour. Once I was inside it, I would open the glove-pocket which invariably contained the same three things: tablets of Corydrane, which against all medical advice he would crunch as dogs crunch lumps of sugar, a blue bottle of Optrex and an enormous cylinder.

Who was my father, really? What used he to do, what does he do now? On the beach at Deauville, last year, when a casual acquaintance asked her what her husband did, my mother replied candidly: 'I have never known.'

Nor have I. I know only scraps, just the surface: a former pupil of the École des Sciences Politiques, a humble clerk in the Dupont bank in Paris, French teacher to an American film star, translator of a Hungarian book (although he never spoke that language), ghost writer for a number of authors whose lectures he prepared, friend and promoter of the Quatre Saisons Theatre company directed by Jean Dasté, founder (before the war) of an *avant-garde* left-wing paper, *L'Ordre Nouveau*; a high-up railway official; a leading Civil Servant, first in the Ministry of Finance and then in Public Works, a member of Laval's staff and French *chargé d'affaires* in Berne, which was then the hub of all European and world-wide conspiracies.

After the war I knew my father as secretary to a Spanish business man at Lausanne, publisher in Geneva, manager of a plastics works at Vevey, promoter of underground railways in several South or North American capital cities, financial go-between for international markets, maintaining mysterious friendships at the Quai d'Orsay and in various ministries, all this without ever making his fortune but, whatever the circumstances and whatever the means at his disposal, always managing to hold his own.

For the last twenty years, although his home-port has been on the shores of the Lake of Geneva, in a villa built around 1900 by the Roussy family, founders of Nestlé's, my father has most frequently slept in the Orient Express. Constantly on the go between Vevey and Paris, his real home is in a sleeping carriage, and by dint of habit I have come to consider the line Paris–Dijon–Vallorbe–Lausanne–Vevey as family property. Accompanying my father on to the platform was like going into his own street, and taking him to his carriage meant seeing him home. He knows the guards in each coach by name. 'His room' is always in the middle, away from the wheels and the creaking of the bogies. In winter he is often the only traveller bound for Paris, and the Paris–Constantinople express—supreme luxury!—seems to halt at Vevey solely for his sake. Out of season, when bookings are few and there's plenty of room, it's not unusual to see one or several friends of ours board the train, armed with nothing but a platform ticket. Crossing the frontier has become a mere formality. One day when my father and I were travelling with Edgar Faure* (who is at home in the Jura) a new policeman at the frontier raised objections because I had forgotten my son's passport. He muttered something about kidnapping. An old customs officer told him: 'It's the Jardin family.' Edgar Faure whistled between his teeth with his customary irony and that mischievous lisp (which reminds me of Michel Audiard's): 'That's power for you!'

✦

7th November 1942. In spite of everything, of the divisions between Frenchmen, of the erosion of power, of hunger, of fear, the outcome of the war and the fate of Vichy were still undecided. Pierre Laval still held trumps which made him a partner rather than a vassal of Germany's, and which enabled him to negotiate, not merely to temporize, with Hitler.

Vichy still kept up diplomatic relations with all neutral countries and even with the enemies of Germany.

* Prime Minister 1952–5. Minister of Agriculture 1966–8, of Education 1968–9, of Social Affairs 1972–3. Now President of National Assembly.

87

Since the armistice, Vichy had an army of a hundred thousand men which could play a decisive role in case of any massive landing of the Allies in the unoccupied zone. Pétain's Government, furthermore, controlled France's colonial empire and in particular her war fleet, which was lying at anchor at Toulon.

8th November. A call on the direct line to Charmeil. My father answered. I was by his side. We must have been among the first French to learn that the Americans had landed in North Africa. From then onwards chaos prevailed. The Americans did not trust General Giraud in Algiers any more than they trusted de Gaulle in London. Weygand, who commanded the troops in North Africa until November 1941 and who was succeeded in the North African territories by the future Marshal Juin, had said: 'If the Americans come with one division I'll chuck them in the water. If they come with twenty I shall embrace them.'

What made things even more fantastically involved was that whereas the French troops in North Africa were strongly anti-German they had none the less remained loyal to Pétain. Hitler, who saw which way the wind was blowing, proposed to Laval, through the intermediary of Krug von Nidda, who represented the German embassy at Vichy, a total alliance for better or worse. After consulting the Marshal for form's sake, Laval refused categorically. Immediately afterwards he broke off diplomatic relations with America in order to remain, as far as possible, neutral. This desperate poker-playing represented the essence of Laval's strategy, a kind of peasant sharp-practice, desperately attempting to reconcile things that were irreconcilable. On learning of Laval's refusal, Hitler summoned him to Munich on the following day, 9th November.

Hour by hour, the situation was becoming impossible to hold, as de Gaulle was to say later of May 1968.

In Algeria, Admiral Darlan temporized with the Americans but put off reaching an agreement. To conclude one with them would mean condemning the unoccupied zone to immediate invasion.

In Munich, Laval was coping single-handed with a completely demented Hitler.

Fearing, not without reason, that he might be arrested and tortured, Laval had provided himself with a phial of cyanide. He was only to use it four years later, in an attempt to escape the French firing squad. Having come to defend France's colonial empire, Laval found it impossible to put in a single word, and Hitler ordered him to prepare Tunisia for an imminent German landing. Laval refused. But what means of defence had he? His everlasting white tie and his fantastic powers of argument. In the apocalyptic maelstrom that was then sweeping over Europe, these were utterly inadequate.

At Vichy, Pétain was very old and very much alone. On all sides he was being urged to take command of the Armistice army and stand up to the occupying forces. Everything was prepared to that end: stores of military equipment were camouflaged close to various centres of resistance. The Jura, the Massif Central and the Alps would provide natural strongholds. The general staff would make its headquarters at Mende, at the centre of operations.

Pétain emerged for the last time from the shadows of his extreme old age. Officially, he ordered Admiral Darlan to repulse the American landing and to defend North Africa against all invaders, including the Germans. Unofficially, he was expecting a telegram from Algiers from General Giraud, who was secretly negotiating with the Americans to try and secure the formal promise of an immediate second landing in the South of France. For the space of a few hours, anything might still happen; the fate of history hung in the balance amid these uneasy, sporadic, unco-ordinated movements between Munich, Vichy and Algiers.

The historical reality was that time was on the side of another man, the man who had one single idea, who never compromised with anyone, who didn't care whether the 'free' zone was occupied or not. He had no love for the French people, he considered them second-rate; he loved only France, his own idea of

France, a terminal idea which disregarded the vicissitudes of fortune.

On 11th November 1942, as though to celebrate in its own fashion the 1918 armistice, the German army invaded the unoccupied zone. At 10.30 that morning Marshal von Rundstedt presented himself at the Hôtel du Parc. All hope gone, pale as death, the Marshal received him, wearing his Verdun uniform, with a single decoration on his breast, the Medaille Militaire—a terrifying, tragic gesture of vanity on the part of a ruined soldier.

Henceforward the whole country was to live under conditions of total occupation. The Nazi jackboot was to spare nothing.

On the morning of 12th November Robert Aron turned up at Charmeil, together with his wife; the Gestapo was on his heels, and he had only managed to shake it off in Vichy itself. There was a humanist dreamer within his giant's frame. My mother considered him the very picture of an intellectual; but I thought he looked like Tarzan. This man, who had initiated the personalist movement in France, who had foreshadowed federalism, was subsequently to become the great historian of the Second World War and its consequences: *Histoire de Vichy, Histoire de la libération de la France, Les Grands Dossiers de l'Histoire contemporaine.*

On that occasion, if I had been asked what his chances of survival were, I'd have said nil. He had been going to leave Marseille by air for Algiers on 8th November, with forged papers provided by my father, made out in the name of Robert Arnaud. The American landing in North Africa resulted in the cancellation of all official flights. He was caught in a trap. I gave up my room to him and took his meals up so that nobody should see him. I don't think I have ever met a man on whom the present had less hold. He never thought that he might be captured, tortured and killed. He thought of nothing concrete. In spite of the increasing cold, against everyone's advice, he would leave the house to go and bathe in the Allier under the very nose of the German officers who were fishing for salmon there. Meanwhile his wife, who is a Basque, was trying to arrange for him to cross the Pyrenees into Spain.

On 13th November the diplomat Krug von Nidda came to lunch at our house. He was a German but not a Nazi. I was sitting at the top of the staircase leading from the drawing-room to the first floor, hidden by a right-angled bend in the stair; I was keeping watch. I could hear Krug von Nidda's ponderous voice explaining to my father that if Laval, who was then in Munich with Hitler, did not agree to help Germany conquer Africa, Germany would do it alone and Hitler would retain possession of the French colonial empire. Furthermore, he dreaded the least sign of resistance in the unoccupied zone. According to him, this would immediately trigger off a process of endless reprisals, the ultimate aim of which might be the dismissal of the existing Government team and its replacement by one totally under German control, with Doriot or Déat at its head, or, worse still, the complete suppression of any French government in France. The country would then be run by a Gauleiter with absolute authority.

A long silence reigned in the drawing-room. I knew beforehand that it would not be broken by my father. His technique was to listen to the end. He never asked questions to which he knew the answers. Finally the voice of one of those present, a Frenchman, spoke up:

'Hitler would never do that.'

Krug von Nidda's answer fell like the blade of a guillotine:

'Who is to stop him?'

A fresh silence, the Krug von Nidda added, more regretfully than by way of a threat:

'Whatever the outcome of the war, it would be the end of France.'

Things had reached that point when somebody walked over me without seeing me, without feeling me, without stopping. It was just Robert Aron going downstairs with his pipe in his mouth to take a walk in the garden. He had simply forgotten that he was a Jew, that he was in hiding in Vichy in late 1942 and that Krug von Nidda was sitting in the drawing-room at the bottom of the stairs.

On seeing him appear, my father was literally struck dumb with horror. Krug von Nidda rose, expecting to be introduced to this stranger who had dropped from the skies. Father sat quite still. Aron smiled in a vague sort of way at the two astonished men, stuck his hands in his pockets and walked quite calmly out of the house. His departure left a kind of emptiness which, for a moment, nothing could fill. Finally Krug von Nidda's voice rang out:

'My dear Jean Jardin, do you remember Disraeli's advice?'

'What was that?'

'Never explain.'

A few days after leaving the house Robert Aron was none the less arrested by the Gestapo. He later escaped and made his way to Algiers, where he played an active part in the work of the Giraud and de Gaulle Governments.

•

27th November 1942. As my brother and I were sitting astride the garden gate, we saw a man making his way on foot towards the house. He walked oddly, zigzagging across the path, reeling like a drunk. After a moment I recognized his face. It was Jean Leroy, a childhood friend of my father's, an expert submariner, who for the past few months had been Principal Private Secretary for the Navy. His jacket was undone; his face was bathed in tears. We asked him questions, but he did not answer, just went on and stood in front of the house and began calling out in a despairing voice: 'Simone, Simone.'

At last Mother came out to meet him, and he collapsed into her arms. She asked him how he had got here? He implied, with a gesture, that he had come on foot. As he just went on weeping silently she tried to find out whether anything had happened to his wife or his children. He shook his head. After a very long pause he simply said: 'The Fleet didn't fight. It has just scuttled itself in Toulon harbour.' And then he fell to his knees and hid his head in his hands.

Thus, between the 7th and the 27th of November 1942, Laval had lost all his trump cards. The unoccupied zone had ceased to exist, the Armistice Army had been dissolved, the Fleet was scuttled. As for the colonial empire, it had broken away. Henceforward Vichy not only had to go on governing between the hammer and the anvil, but to do so empty-handed. Its political defeat was complete. This was the implacable beginning of a long death-agony.

◆

Christmas 1942. At dawn, in the bitter cold, I went to inspect the shoes I had left beside the drawing-room fireplace. They were empty. A friend who was visiting us, Yves de Chomereau, Inspecteur des Finances, a very tall, alarmingly thin man who suffered terribly from asthma, emerged from the armchair in which he had taken refuge when driven from his bed by choking fits. Tears were streaming from his left eye. I knew why. Dr. Giraudoux had given him some horrible injections in the eyes to check the asthma. He sat down at the piano, played Bach and Mozart, and explained to me that all Father Christmases were on strike and that their protest movement in favour of peace had affected almost every chimney in Europe. I listened to him while I put on my shoes. In one of them I found a visiting card with a few lines scribbled on it. Yves de Chomereau deciphered them for me. It was a message from Mme Eisenmann, whom my father had rescued from the German police, saying that an electric train had been delivered at our home in Paris. It was later sent to my grandparents' at Bernay, and eventually stolen at the Liberation by members of the F.F.I. (French Forces of the Interior)* who were keen on model railways.

I dragged Yves de Chomereau, who seemed to be in a bad way, into the kitchen, where I made him some coffee. That

---

* i.e. the Resistance.

gloomy Christmas morning, sitting beside the stove, I learned a strange story which reassured me somewhat about myself. As a child, in a stable on his father's country estate, Chomereau had come upon one of the maids being forcibly embraced by the coachman. The girl, who was young and pretty, had a bandage round her ankle. Since then, he had always fancied women with bandaged ankles more than any others. I was amazed, and told him about Florence and her boots. He was deeply touched; we felt like two brothers. He took me back into the drawing-room, transformed the grand piano into a harpsichord by sticking drawing-pins into the felt hammers, and played sarabands and minuets until he had woken up the entire household.

After lunch, my mother made both her sons wash from head to foot. Then Simon and I put on flannel suits of the kind small boys wore in the thirties. Thus togged out, we set forth in a family party for the big house, the Château de Charmeil, where Marshal Pétain was expecting us.

I only have a rather dim memory of that official party. Mother didn't know what to say to Madame la Maréchale, who said nothing at all. Father and I walked round the park with the Marshal, who was in civilian dress and kept twirling his stick about with great brilliance. He told us a story from his days as a young cavalry officer:

'I reined in my horse and rose up in my stirrups; I called out through a megaphone: "Don't ride through the potatoes." Then the subaltern who was leading the charge turned back to tell me: "They're not potatoes, they're turnips." '

And then the Marshal raised his stick heavenwards like a stern avenging angel:

'Turnips, good Lord! Forward then, the lot of you!'

That's a tiny piece of evidence about the victor of Verdun. It's the only one I have'.

Late January 1943. The road leading to the village school was frozen hard. My wooden-soled shoes clattered like the beating of a drum. In my short pants, my calves blue with cold and my nose muffled in a woollen scarf, on I went. Like Sartre's hero

94

in *Les Mains Sales*, I was not hungry; like him, while France was starving I was overfed, and I had in my pocket tablets of Nestrovite, that khaki-coloured vitaminized chocolate provided by the Red Cross. I was well aware of the bloodshed and devastation in the world around me; I had learnt from my grown-up acquaintances, from those who were being hunted down and those who ate caviar at Maxim's, from English friends and from German friends, from profiteers and from victims, that we were living through a crucial time. And what part was I playing in all this? I wanted my share of money and misfortune. I wanted to lose an arm, to win a medal, I wanted to go to prison, to shed blood, to be somebody. Everything except:

'Three times three? Come on dear, what is three multiplied by three?'

'I don't see, Madame.'

'You mean you don't know, I suppose?'

'No, I don't see.'

'What don't you see?'

'I don't see anything.'

'But it's broad daylight!'

'Not for me.'

It would have been too easy to accept one's smallness, one's need of protection. I was so afraid of coming to enjoy my childhood that I rejected it out of hand.

The school was housed in a superb eighteenth-century building. That day the teacher had made us wash our hands and comb our mops of hair. My friend Georges Hilaire, Minister of Fine Arts, was to pay us a visit. He really was my friend. I was on the freest of terms with all dreamy childless intellectuals. Fathers of families always maintain an almost racist prejudice towards children. Whereas Georges Hilaire would ask me whether I liked sunflowers, or mutton stew, or going to the cinema. Nobody had told him I was a child, so he did not realize it. Possibly he even took me for a dwarf.

When he came into the school the blushing teacher made us all stand up, and at her word of command we struck up in chorus, without knowing why: 'Marshal, we are here before you, saviour of France . . .'* He listened absent-mindedly to this politico-social top-of-the-pops. He was quite clearly bored. What interested him here was not the pupils but the construction of the roof, which had been carried out from a design by Nicolas Ledoux. Just as he was about to vanish, under our teacher's guidance, up the staircase that led into the loft, I lost my head and shouted at the top of my voice: 'Get me out of here, I can't stand it.' The teacher nearly fainted. Georges Hilaire, taken aback, looked round the class and finally recognized me. He seemed astonished at finding me here, as though the official in charge of galley-slaves had found his spiritual son and heir chained to the bench. Forgetful of his surroundings and of the swarming presence of forty urchins, he replied coldly:

'I can't do anything for you, ask Abel Bonnard!'

A few days later my guardian Minister came to dine with us at Charmeil. He was accompanied by M. Motono, Japanese ambassador to Vichy, and his wife, a plump little yellow person with narrowed slits of eyes and a porcelain smile.

Abel Bonnard was a small man, precious and precise, with a fuzz of white hair. A member of the French Academy, a poet in his spare time and a Minister through some misunderstanding, he belonged to that unhappy category of homosexuals who adore women and hate being men. Really, he would have liked to be a Lesbian. He was one of those whom the legal polemicist Stephen Hecquet was later to describe with his usual savagery as 'incapable of inserting, unfitted for receiving, just a roving hand.' I was introduced to this elderly pansy.

'My boy, how is your writing?'

'I can't write, Monsieur le Ministre.'

'Can you read?'

'Not at all.'

'Can you count?'

'I'm afraid not.'

* *Maréchal, nous voilà* . . . the official anthem of Vichy France.

The pathetic old queen with mascaraed eyes gave me a melting glance and tut-tutted asthmatically.

'But what do you know, then?'

Silence fell. Thirty people were watching me. I was alone facing my fate, which was nothingness.

'I don't know anything, Monsieur le Ministre.'

'Nothing at all?'

'Absolutely nothing.'

Tears rose to his eyes. One of them even trickled down his baby-soft cheek. He hugged me and congratulated me. If he'd had a Legion of Honour rosette by him he'd have fastened it behind my ear, or even on my flies. He was torn between pederastic lyricism and a predilection for paradox. Turning to the two Japs, he remarked:

'Heavens, how rare it is in this delusively enlightened age to meet a young creature whose mind is still unperverted by any learning. I am paying tribute not to his ignorance but to his virginity.'

M. Motono grew yellower and yellower. He seemed ready for another Pearl Harbor.

About midnight the Apostolic Nuncio arrived. He was a prelate out of a Fellini film, clad in a tight silk cassock cut by Jeanne Lanvin. He was in a tizzy at the thought of being best man at the wedding of Danielle Darrieux and Rubirosa.

That night, again, the house was astir until dawn. In the immense drawing-room, my mother played the piano. Father was glued to the telephone, calling Paris, Berne, Bucharest. In the upstairs rooms, friends whose lives were in danger waited for a pirate aircraft to carry them to Algiers, or for forged papers for Spain, or for the end of the war . . .

✦

6th October 1969. My memory is a swamp. Hitherto I have only put up a few wild ducks and dodged some snakes. Now I'm getting bogged down. A black hole is yawning. I know what has become of the men and women I used to know at Vichy. They are dead, or ruined, or exiled, or else in power, some flourishing, some remarried, some grandmothers, some invalids. But what has time done to the house itself, that house at Charmeil whose picture is as firmly fixed in my mind as though it had been soldered inside my head?

I know it by heart, the size of the drawing-room, the number of windows, the colour of the walls, the slope of the roof, the layout of the garden; I was quite old when I left it at the age of nine and a half, on 31st October 1943; and I have never been back to it. What has become of it? Was it burnt down, demolished, has it become a bourgeois dwelling, a holiday home, a service station? Is it huge only in my memory? Does there still linger in the neighbouring fields, in the trees in the garden, in the air that surrounds it any reflection, any redolence, any echo of what I have been describing and of what I still want to call back into life? A hundred times I have felt a wish, and even had the opportunity, to go to Vichy and find out. And each time I have shirked going. Charmeil is something more for me; it's my lighthouse, my retreat, my only true home.

7th October 1969. 8 a.m. I made up my mind. I got on the phone to my father in Switzerland. He could not recall the name of our landlord; he only remembered that the man was a lawyer with a practice at Cusset. I rang up the various legal men in that neighbourhood. Eventually I found out that the house still existed and that it belonged to the widow of a solicitor. I succeeded in speaking to this woman, who also lived at Cusset. I explained to her as best I could that I was writing a book of recollections, and I begged her to let me revisit, that very day, the house where I had lived as a child. She was astonished and suspicious, unable to understand my strange craving to pay an immediate visit to a country house built in the twenties, quite lacking in character, without even the distinction of ugliness, and in her view offering not the slightest interest. But what sort of condition was it in? Fearing lest our telephone talk should give her a bad impression of me, I persuaded her to let me pick her up at her home at three o'clock that afternoon. I hung up, I got out my car, and swept at record speed through Nemours, Montargis, Nevers and Moulins; I reached Vichy less than six hours after my first exploratory phone call. I stopped to get my breath in the very centre of the town, outside the baths. Ten yards away, the Hôtel du Parc, the seat of Laval's government, had been sold as flats. The town was dead. The imperial lodges built by Napoleon III for his suite, which during the war had served as embassies or legations, seemed closed for all eternity. The Majestic, next to the Hôtel du Parc, had been sold too. It was like Nice in winter, but without the sea. I suddenly felt a conviction that nothing would ever bring this drowned city back to life. Few towns are called upon twice to play a part in political history. I got back into the car, drove to Cusset, passed Louis XI's house and located that of the solicitor's widow. She received me: a sad provincial lady of fifty. I took her on board and we drove across the Allier by the Boutiron bridge. Six kilometres further on we entered the village of Charmeil. It was chock-full of new buildings. I found this somehow reassuring. What I was dreading and hoping for must no longer exist in its old form. I drove past the Marshal's château on my right; it had been turned into a hostelry for Pétinist pilgrims. I took the Saint-Pourcin road: there was my school, intact, on the left. The discomfort this aroused was quickly banished, for on my right, the marshland on the banks of the Allier, where the small semi-clandestine airfield used to be, had become an annexe of Orly. A control tower, bristling with radar posts, kept watch for the Algerian and Moroccan Boeings that used it as a half-way landing place. The nearer we got to 'my house' the more reassured I felt. Time had done its work. Here, the past was not slumbering, it was dead. Sitting by my side, the solicitor's widow kept up a monotonous chant on an outmoded theme: 'If you only knew, Monsieur . . . that inheritance . . . joint ownership . . . it hasn't even been let since nineteen forty-four.'

Although I had not listened much to the beginning, this last sentence chilled my blood, just as I saw the house appear on my left, rather high up, barely visible—the house, secret, shut, forgotten, preserved. I repeat, I *saw* the house just as I heard the words 'not let since nineteen forty-four', the act of seeing coinciding with the abstract idea.

The car climbed swiftly up the road leading to the front gate. This was open. Nettles a yard high obstructed the drive. On the left, a telegraph post called up a forgotten memory: two of the Marshal's motor-cycle outriders shooting down an old peasant. He had died there, before my eyes, without saying a word, with his back to the post against which they had stood him. I drove over nettles and turned right. The box edging of the terrace must have grown in a quarter of a century from one to four or five metres high. I got out of the car and opened the second gate. I went in. I knew that I was close to the root of a real emotion. On this early October afternoon in 1969 the weather was radiant, as it had been in June 1942. The house was empty. All the furniture had been removed, but the wallpaper had not changed, nor the stair-carpet, nor the bathroom on the first floor, nor the cylindrical leather thongs that controlled the Venetian blinds, nor the mirrors. I went into my parents' bedroom. Here, semi-darkness reigned. Close to the door, low down on the left, on the plinth, supported by rusty metal rings, were the cut-off ends of three pieces of wire, which had belonged to our private telephone. I crouched down and took the wires in my hand. They were corroded. These lines, connected with a moment in history, were silent for ever: there was nobody to call or to answer. Pierre Laval had been shot. Philippe Pétain had died on the Île d'Yeu. Marshal Rommel had been 'suicided' by the Gestapo. Jean Giraudoux was dead; Drieu la Rochelle had killed himself; Brasillach had been shot. Through these old bits of rusty copper that were crumbling away between my fingers, the first news of world events had come, by day or by night: the American landing in North Africa, the scuttling of the fleet at Toulon, the invasion of the unoccupied zone . . .

I went up to the french window that gave on to the balcony. I flung it open. I pulled up the blinds. The sun streamed in. I turned round, and in that bare room I saw, not memories of gestures or faces, but something impossible to look at—I saw how beautiful my mother had been at that time.

I stayed there ten minutes and then I went back to Paris.

•

Spring 1943. A tiny car drew up in front of the steps. At first nothing happened, and then a gigantic person unfolded himself and emerged from his nutshell. It was my cousin Edmond Duchesne, mayor of Honfleur. He weighed a hundred kilos. He had the elephantine charm of Babar. He had come to spend the day at Vichy to see Laval. My brother and I pestered him to take us back to spend a fortnight in Normandy. My parents agreed, and we settled down in the back of his Simca.

From Vichy to Pacy-sur-Eure, nothing happened. Just as we were about to start the run down into Evreux my brother called out, pointing to the sky: 'We're done for, *grand cousin*.' I leaned out of the window. Over our heads the sky was full of Flying Fortresses. Not just a hundred planes, but a whole armada of them making at top speed for the Evreux airfield, some five hundred metres behind us. Through the back window I could see on the runway, parallel with the road, Messerschmitts taking off at a terrifying rate. We came to an emergency halt on a little bridge, where the flying club is nowadays. We dashed under the bridge and watched things happening. The German flak surrounded the bombers with little rosy clouds. One German fighter, hit in mid-flight, lost a wing, came spiralling down leaving a superb black tornado behind it and finally burst into red flames. At that stage of the war, Americans bombing German objectives still found it a risky business. These formidable airborne tanks were vulnerable; once hit, they did not fall immediately. I had time to see some men jump. One of them was carried by the wind in our direction; he was tugging at the ropes of his parachute so as to fall as far as possible from the German base. Just as he was about to touch ground a storm of machine-gun fire caught him; he crumpled up in the air and collapsed like a burst bag less than fifty metres away from us.

All this, however, was just a prelude. The earth opened up, flew into the air. It had turned into clouds of dust. We couldn't see a thing. For a moment it seemed as if night had fallen. When light came back the Flying Fortresses had disappeared. The air-field had gone. Behind us, the road to Paris along which we had just driven had been torn open over more than a kilometre. We climbed back into the Simca. I was deafened and dazzled. I had not been frightened; I hadn't had time.

When we entered Evreux ten minutes later, the sky was once again black with bombers. This time they really were less than a hundred metres over our heads. These planes had taken off from British bases near the coast. As they were going deep into Germany to drop their bombs on the industrial Ruhr, they rose very slowly so as to economise on fuel and thus have a chance of getting back to England. They were heavily loaded, and every inch of metal vibrated. The throb of their over-heated engines set the whole town quivering in a sort of St. Vitus's dance that affected the inhabitants as well as the houses and their contents.

We drew up in the Rue de la Préfecture, at the home of my maternal grandfather, Dr. Duchesne. The hall, the drawing-room and the cellar were crammed full of people who had taken refuge there. A few stray bombs had fallen on the town, starting fires. Fire engines tore down the streets. People were running in all directions. Germans were barking out orders. Grandfather and Grandmother, in white coats, were tending the injured who were lying all over the place. It wasn't a house any more, it was a field hospital. I threaded my way through a maze of piled-up furniture and human wrecks moaning and weeping. I made for the garden. Turning to look at the house, I realized that part of it was missing. Looking closer, I had to admit that half of it was missing. As my room gave on to the part that had disappeared I went up to the second floor and opened my cupboard. There were no more coats hanging there, just sheer emptiness and a splendid view over the ruined town.

Before going to bed I went for a walk with Monsieur Père as far as the cathedral. It had lost its biggest, finest tower. All the medieval houses that used to stand round it had vanished. We went forward through a heap of ruins; even the layout of the streets was no longer recognizable. People were living like moles, camping out in tumble-down cellars. There was no electric light anywhere, but a sumptuous full moon lit up this scene of desolation. A German patrol stopped us roughly. Monsieur Père showed his doctor's pass, which authorized him to be out after curfew. We went home together in silence. Up there in the sky we could hear the Allied aircraft flying off tirelessly to pound Nazi Germany. I felt cold. My own town, my mother's town, had no face any more.

Next morning we left for Honfleur. The city was intact. But no sooner had we arrived than an infernal banging began. A colossal bomb nose-dived into the old harbour, just beside the caravel which had been turned into a place of amusement. Fortunately the harbour had not been dredged for twenty years. Fifteen feet of mud saved us from an explosion.

When night came, I watched Le Havre burning for the second time from the terrace of the Duchesne cousins' huge house overlooking the estuary. The RAF fighters performed fantastic loops in the beams of the German searchlights. The British were fighting one against ten. When one has seen them bringing down Messerschmitts like ninepins one understands why Hitler never succeeded in invading Britain. It was the first time I had seen heroes. These were unforgettable. About once an hour the sky boomed over our heads and a steel monster spewing out flames rent the darkness with a hissing sound, as if the world were coming to an end. It was the V 1s and V 2s of Herr von Braun, future boss of NASA, on their way to set London ablaze.

✦

Deauville was no longer Deauville. There were no more chocolates being sold on the bare boards of the Marquise de Sévigné sweet-shop. The window was just a gaping hole, and there were machine-guns firing instead of lollies. Behind the bathing huts, the Club des Canards had become a building site where an indestructible casemate was being finished; it's still there. The fantastic Todt organization had left its mark everywhere, even in the Bar du Soleil. As far as the eye could reach, from Villers to Le Havre, the concrete tents of war were spread out. The beach was criss-crossed with trenches and barbed wire. The receding tide uncovered strings of mines half-buried in the sand. Everywhere bilingual notices warned one that bathing, parking, laughter and happiness were *verboten*. On the grass in front of the Casino stood tanks and guns guarded by soldiers who were quite unlike those I had seen arrive in the Vendee at the beginning of the war. These men were not good-looking, they were not young, they were not cheerful.

As the situation had become too chancy, my Honfleur cousin would not undertake the responsibility of keeping us any longer. Having neither time nor enough petrol to drive us home, he managed to ring up Vichy and tell my father he would take us as far as Evreux, to our grandparents'.

During this brief journey we stopped at Breuil-Pont for lunch with his mother-in-law, a delightful fresh-faced old lady who lived in a dream-house with a cottage garden.

What I saw that day I shall never forget. We had been sitting at table some ten minutes when the sky began to rumble. We went out and looked up; an air battle was going on, the sort of thing one gets used to. The objective of the Allied bombers was fairly close to us, it was the German ordnance depot at Arnière-sur-Iton. But since this time the battle was taking place at a very high altitude, there was no sort of precision about the bombing and everything came down on top of us. The noise was so intense that it quickly became like a sort of silence. A German fighter plane which had lost its tail came plunging down towards the house. We all fled in disorder through the apple orchard. But the aircraft righted itself, avoided us and flew away to collapse further off. I went back into the house.

All the furniture was dancing. Sideboards and dressers were jigging about, groaning in every hinge. Doors flew open, and the clock struck. The plates of old Rouen china hanging on the wall fell down and were smashed. It was lively, but deafening. When the cyclone had moved on the grown-ups present set up a feeble lamentation. Their comments were vapid, their complaints utterly trivial. Not so much a commentary on the Gallic wars, more a set of comic-strip captions. I walked out on these unreal bourgeois and made my way through the long grass, under the apple trees, as far as the wash-house. I looked at the river. It was a lovely day, on the verge of summer. But suddenly the water grew cloudy, it changed colour, it turned reddish, it became blood-red. And then there appeared pieces of human beings. The river bore them along like a moving tray, all sorts: bare feet, shod feet, heads, hands, bundles of innards, tangles of viscera, bodies caught up in tufts of watercress. The bits that were still clothed were clothed in green cloth. Germany had cut Europe into pieces and here, before my eyes, was the prefiguration of the mincemeat the Allies would have to make of Hitler's armies in order to silence them. A helmet sailed down all on its own, a funny little boat spinning round like a top in the eddies.

I went back through the apple trees to the house. I don't know if I was frightened. I couldn't speak. They offered me half a lump of sugar and a slice of black bread by way of dessert. I put them in my pocket. I was really not hungry.

When I got to Evreux Madame Mère was delighted. Father had told her he was leaving us in her charge for a whole week. The chief occupation of the entire family consisted in watching for air-raid warnings. As soon as the siren started we plunged into the cellar, which was deep and dirty. Nights seemed endless in that unhealthy place which reeked of cider and old dead rats.

'If the house collapses and the cellar holds, we shall all die of hunger,' Monsieur Père declared.

Madame Mère, draped in a checked blanket and looking like a bad-tempered Indian chief, shut him up by calling him an idiot and a shirker. In any case, she didn't think we could die of hunger. She'd had a ventilator giving on to the garden enlarged so that we could crawl out if need be. Unfortunately the opening was so small that only the cat could have taken advantage of it. My aunt, who was far gone in pregnancy and panic-stricken at the sound of the bombs, had another theory which she kept repeating, nearly sick with mounting terror: 'When a house falls down the gas pipes burst and the people inside are always gassed.'

I soon took a violent dislike to the cellar. While the warnings were on I would stay in the garden and shout down alarmist messages to my family of moles.

One evening when the sky was calm and my grandmother's poor heart was not thumping too hard, the two of us went for a short walk before curfew. We had got as far as the Rue Chartraine when I heard a terrible noise behind me. She hugged me close to her; the end of her scarf tickled my nose. A big German truck had just collided with a car. It drove on erratically and finally came to a halt in the window of a dress shop, where it became firmly embedded. We went closer. Frightful cries were coming from inside the truck. An ambulance appeared very quickly. The driver of the truck was unhurt but the young soldiers who were sitting at the back between cases of munitions had been crushed. They were carried away on stretchers. One of them had his back broken in two. He was screaming. I could see he did not want to die.

At the far end of my grandparents' garden, the other side of a stream which was fifteen feet across, you could see the grounds of a villa belonging to friends of our family and occupied by the Kommandatur. On the roof there flew a huge flag with a swastika. By day it was impossible to spy there because the sentries walking up and down the paths ordered me to scram as soon as they caught sight of me. But at night I could crouch down by the side of the stream and wait. The most disturbing rumours were rife about that accursed place. Madame Mère told me that Frenchmen were tortured there by day and by night. Monsieur Père had been sent for, once, to attend to a man whose eye had been put out.

106

One evening when I was at my post I heard a great hullabaloo and shouting. Then a man in shirtsleeves came out by a ground-floor french window. He was running as hard as he could. Germans ran after him and shot at him and he fell. The Germans picked him up and carried him back. Was I frightened, disgusted, horrified? I don't know. Since the beginning of the war I had heard so much talk of death that the actual sight of it did not impress me. Next day the whole town had heard of the incident. Everybody knew that a hundred yards from Dr. Duchesne's garden, a hundred yards from the old weeping ash in which my brother and I had built a hut, people were having their nails torn off, were being maimed, were being killed. Everybody knew this, everybody kept silent about it, nobody stirred. Insidiously, I learned from the adults around me my lesson of silence and cowardice.

•

Turnips are nicer with sausage. Uncle Paul has lost Titine. Important, we repeat, Uncle Paul has lost Titine. Bent over the huge radio set which she called 'my wireless', Madame Mère was listening to the coded messages sent out by Radio-London. As the Germans tried to jam them, a frantic caterwauling interfered with the reception. One of the maids came in fuming; she had washed her face with soap made by Madame Mère from ivy leaves out of the garden, and now it was as pock-marked as Mirabeau's. Madame Mère consoled her:

'It's nothing, girl, just a bad reaction, it'll all be gone by tomorrow.'

'But Madame, my boy-friend . . .'

'He's a German. You just give him your spots and tell him from me to pass them on to Hitler.'

'Very well, Madame.'

The maid went out, subdued. In came Helmut Sharptnelle—I write it just as I pronounce it, badly. He was one of the two German N.C.O.s who had requisitioned rooms on our second floor. He seemed very worried.

'Matame Duchesne-Doktor, Radio-London verboten.'

My grandmother knew nothing of any foreign languages except the inscriptions on railway carriage windows. So she barked at him fiercely:

'E pericoloso sporgersi. Raus!'

And he, the conqueror, unaware that he would some day frequent the Club Méditerranée, stupidly persisted.

'Matame, dangerous. Police car trap, ja!'

'Ja, ja, with an umbrella spinning on the roof. I know the two twerps who are sitting inside it with earphones. I've helped my husband flush out their ears—full of wax, filthy pigs, must be Prussians! Raus!'

Disgusted, this representative of the occupying army left the dining-room and went off to find his spotty girl-friend. He was so fed up with his landlady that he was ready to ask for a suicidal posting to the Eastern front. Hidden behind the tapestry curtains, with their patterns of forests haunted by nightmarish devils and unicorns, I was watching people go in and out of the dining-room, disturbing Madame Mère at her task of Resistance-movement monitoring. I was enjoying myself madly. War is fun when you're only nine, even though the town was in flames and everybody was dying of hunger. Monsieur Père and Madame Mère had lost twenty-nine kilos between them. Fresh from Vichy where I'd been well fed, I felt a little ashamed in front of all these old folks who were grey with worry and exhaustion. London fell silent. With a flick of her experienced thumb Madame Mère switched over to Radio-Paris. A quavering voice sounded on the wheezy waves. Could it be the Marshal? No, it was Martini, a *chansonnier*. He sounded awfully pro-German and shrill; Madame Mère was disgusted, and hurled invective at her radio set. Then Monsieur Père came in, bringing a treat—a real Camembert! Night fell. In the street, Germans were marching past.

Attracted by the smell of the cheese—in those precarious days, news of food travelled as swiftly as swallows skimming low in bad weather—the curé of Saint-Taurin church turned up for dinner. Monsieur Père was an atheist, Madame Mère had given up God in despair when the clergy had robbed her by buying for next to nothing the land on which they built the prodigiously profitable basilica of Lisieux.

I was fond of this priest, who talked to me about Bach as one might talk about Tarzan. He was in an impossible situation. He was a genuinely religious man, who took his vows of poverty seriously. He was consequently suspected of subversion by the local bourgeoisie. Being non-political, he took no active part in the Resistance; being courageous, he sheltered the hunted. The Germans had their eye on him, so had the collaborators who had failed to enlist him. The poor, too, looked askance at him, because the rich had told them he was an anarchist. Rejected by the clerical Left and by the Church of the rich, by Communists and reactionaries, by the Resistance movement and the occupying forces, he had against him every known ideology in the whole department. Nobody took his side except a few isolated individuals whom he had helped or understood. Madame Mère comforted him by berating him:

'That'll teach you to bother about souls.'

'Oh yes, Madame . . .'

'But it's your business?'

'Oh yes, Madame . . .'

When the meal was over Monsieur Père picked up his stick and put on his hat to go to the hospital, where patients were expecting him. Madame Mère caught up with him on the stairs.

'Robert, your *ausweis*?'

He searched his pockets and admitted:

'It's on my desk.'

'The way you go on you'll get yourself deported! You forget everything, even me!'

'Hélène, my dear . . .'

'None of that nonsense. Look out for bomb craters, you might twist your ankle.'

Monsieur Père, somewhat melancholy, set off to see his patients. Madame Mère went into her kitchen, where she was to spend part of the night concocting shortbread biscuits out of boiled milk skin. When she had finished she would put them into empty medicine containers which she would seal with sealing-wax and dispatch to Germany to relatives in prison camps.

Meanwhile I stayed with the curé, who was smoking cigarettes made of lime-flowers rolled in toilet paper. An hour later, having devoured a whole bowlful of cherries in brandy, he gave me a lecture on French history which was as savage as it was unexpected:

'Madame de Maintenon was a bitch!'

'What d'you mean?'

'As she grew older she lapsed into a religious bigotry which was as different from real faith as aeroplanes are from sailing ships. She made Louis XIV into a sinister figure, and she did worse than that: she reduced Jansenism to orthodoxy, she perverted everything, transforming cruises into crusades, fasting into Swedish gymnastics and virtue into lugubrious melancholy. Since then everything's gone wrong, France has become a country of snivelling children in search of a father-figure. Yesterday it was General Boulanger, today it's Pétain, tomorrow it'll be that long sausage.'

'What long sausage?'

'De Gaulle.'

An appalling din interrupted the visionary priest. Madame Mère had just knocked over the preserving-vessel, a sort of box with walls of quadruple thickness, in which, apparently, one could keep eggs for up to six months in a yellowish liquid . . .

That was my holiday in Normandy, in the spring of 1943.

◆

Vichy. Summer 1943. I lay under a bramble bush by the side of our drive, looking out for Prime Minister Pierre Laval, who was expected for lunch.

I had been there for over an hour without moving when a rumble was heard. I could see a whole convoy coming slowly along the road, in the distance.

The first to leave the main road and veer up the drive towards me were two motor-cyclists armed with machine-guns slung round their necks. Acting as scouts for the convoy, they covered the sixty metres of the drive in a few seconds, rushed past me with a noise like thunder and took up their stand on the raised terrace in front of the house.

Between two open Delahayes crammed with plain-clothes policemen armed to the teeth, there advanced a black monster of over four tons, swaying clumsily on its thick unpuncturable tyres. This machine, which seemed part Rolls-Royce part Panzer, was an armoured Renault, built pre-war for the Queen of England, who had used it on one occasion only, for a visit to Versailles.

Behind the blue-tinted bullet-proof windows I made out, for the first time, the man who was everybody's enemy, whom Marshal Pétain had had arrested on 13th December 1940, who had already had two bullet wounds on 27th August 1941 and had recovered from them, the man who was hated by de Gaulle, by the English, by the Americans and by the Germans too, the doomed man, the man all on his own. This sixty-year-old Auvergnat had the face of a South American peon crossed with an Asiatic, whence his nickname Don Pedro. His narrow eyes and his yellow skin suggested that the Mongol invasion had actually reached the heart of France. By his side sat his daughter Josée, a lean, highly strung, gipsyish beauty. By a curious irony of fate she is an honorary citizen of the United States through her husband, Comte René de Chambrun, a direct descendant of Lafayette.

As soon as their car had passed I cut across the fields and reached the terrace at the same time as they did. Laval's cops leapt out of the Delahayes. Some of them surrounded the armoured Renault, others scattered swiftly through the garden and the house. All of them had weapons in their hands and the faces of professional killers. The chauffeur opened the rear door, and Josée de Chambrun got out of the car, followed by the Prime Minister. As he set foot on the ground I noticed that he was wearing boots of fine black kid with cloth uppers and small mother-of-pearl buttons. He had on a light-coloured suit and, of course, a white tie. He spoke to my father, who came to welcome him, in a harsh sing-song voice. The fingers of his right hand, holding a smouldering American cigarette, were stained with nicotine. His glance fell on me. He stared at me for a moment and then looked at my father, as though to make quite sure whose son I was. After which he gave me a long smile. This fleeting, first, last, only contact with Pierre Laval was interrupted by the regal arrival on the terrace of an enormous open black Mercedes. In the back, on bright red leather cushions, sat a huge man, M. Rahn, the German minister.

I never saw Pierre Laval again and yet his shadow has dominated and conditioned more than half of my life. Because my father had worked for him my schoolfellows at the Evreux *lycée*, later on, spat in my face and beat me up. I can still hear them ask: 'How many Jews did you denounce?'

Shortly after the war, on my way from Switzerland to stay with my grandparents at Evreux, I met in the Rue Las Cases in Paris an important man whose name I shall withhold. He picked me up and kissed me, and said: 'We'll look after your mother, your brother and yourself, but as for your father I shall have him hanged.' I was twelve years old.

If my first wife's parents never wanted me as a son-in-law it was largely because I was the son of a 'collabo'. All in all, if I'd wanted to forget Pierre Laval I could not have done so. For ten or twelve years after the end of the war I was constantly being reminded who I was. It was no easier for me to ignore my childhood than for a Jew to forget, during the war, that he was Jewish.

For a long time I was not unwilling to accept the cut-and-dried notion that Laval was a swine, a '*salaud*' as some French Algerians consider de Gaulle. The insult seemed to me the reverse side of an exceptional destiny, the price paid for that unpardonable fault, political failure. But who was he really? My father never talked to me about him. He never talks about people of whom he has been really fond. The more books I read about this period, which are inevitably about Laval, the more the evidence seems to conflict, even down to details. Some of his acquaintances saw in him a slovenly unkempt fellow, always covered with cigarette ash. Others assert just as categorically that he was a man of real elegance and refinement. Far from lying midway between these two contradictory opinions, the truth must be that Laval was naturally several different people. At that period, indeed, he must have been a whole host of successive and sometimes incompatible characters. So I assume that, depending on the day and the situation, his external appearance must have varied. In the same way I believed for a long time that he had gambled on Germany quite deliberately, whereas in fact from 1940 onwards he no longer controlled his own fate, he had no choice to make, but gradually became involved in an irreversible situation which forced this Parliamentary strategist to play a part which was not really his, the part of a manoeuvrer, and to end up in 1945 as a national traitor. At what point did a man of this sort cease to make use of events and become their victim? Why did he come back from Spain right at the end of the war, when he might have avoided doing so? If Talleyrand, at a certain moment in his life, had not left for the United States, he would probably have been shot too. There is always a propitious moment for making your come-back in politics; why did he choose the most unfavourable one? In order to face the verdict of the French people after four years of war, occupation and deportation? To accept responsibility for his failure and live out his destiny to the end? I don't believe that such men as Laval ever behave like Antigone.

But the real question, which again is unanswerable, goes further back, to the start of things. In politics, where nothing counts but results, how could a tactician of his calibre have landed himself in Vichy when by the end of 1941 London offered a more favourable political future? Why had a man of such foresight consented to play the role of Iago? Pierre Fresnay once told me: 'You can't have Othello without Iago, but you must never play Iago.'

'But then if nobody wants to play the part, who's it for?'

'For other people.'

For a long time, too, I thought of Laval as a right-wing man, his terror of Bolshevism being the thing that held together his pro-German policy. Actually he was very left-wing and before being repeatedly Prime Minister he had begun his career as ultra-Socialist mayor of the 'red' suburb of Aubervilliers. A former friend of his, an old-time Communist, recently explained to me that Laval had wanted to provide post-war France with a Socialist régime so advanced that it would never be in danger of going over to a totalitarian one. Was this not the impracticable 'third way' on which de Gaulle, too, foundered?

Finally, I had thought Laval was a Cartesian rationalist, whereas I now know that he frequented clairvoyants and fortune-tellers. Never having succeeded in finding out anything precise either about my wife, whom I can watch from morning till night, nor even about my children, although they're growing up under my nose and make no attempt to hide anything from me, I have given up trying to form a clear opinion of Pierre Laval. About him, as about everybody else, I just have a mass of impressions, a great many questions to which nobody knows the answers, save perhaps my father. But my father won't speak. He has never accepted publishers' offers and he has rejected all invitations from American weeklies; his secrets will die with him.

That day, about three in the afternoon, after the lunch with Rahn, Pierre Laval and his escort left Charmeil. As soon as they had disappeared I ventured into the drawing-room. Here I found Rahn telling my mother, in perfect French, about his childhood in Berlin after the '14–'18 war. I crept out again terrified on hearing him say that between the ages of seven and eighteen he wept with hunger almost every night.

The evening was to prove more bracing. Rahn and the minister Jacques Leroy-Ladurie sat down at the piano after dinner. The two giants improvised duets. They played mock Bach, mock Mozart, jazzed-up Bach, Beethoven à la Louis Armstrong, with such vehemence that the strings of the piano snapped one after the other. It was repaired next day by a piano-tuner carrying a white stick, who professed to be blind and who stuffed the huge body of our concert Pleyel with quantities of microphones. The trouble with that sort of fellow was that one never knew whether they were working for the Resistance or the Gestapo.

About midnight my father accompanied Rahn to his Mercedes. I followed them. As he was about to get into the car Rahn said in a melancholy tone: 'What do you think would happen if I told them in Berlin what I have heard today?' As my father did not reply, glancing at the chauffeur, Rahn added: 'He doesn't speak French.' Then he got into the car and barked out an order in German, contrasting strangely with his way of expressing himself in French. The fabulous car moved off and disappeared into the night.

✦

Fear settled in everywhere, even at Charmeil. All sorts of strange people came prowling round the house. Father decided to engage three plain-clothes policemen to protect his family. I don't know where these sleuths came from, but they had the most perfect gangsters' mugs ever seen on the movies. They camped out in the garage, surrounded with a formidable array of guns. All night I heard them walking about under my windows. At dawn, exasperated, I stupidly yelled out: 'Who's there? Halt or I fire.' They went in a fury to complain to my mother, explaining that if I got myself shot I'd only have myself to blame. At the end of a week my mother, my brother and I were so terrorized by our guardian angels that we persuaded Father to send them home. The brutes packed up and left. We never saw them again. Apparently they were replaced by members of the Resistance movement who were kindly disposed towards us. The advantage of these friendly partisans over the horrible cops was that one never saw them.

The reaction against war and anguish seemed to be a frenzy

for living at any price, at an ever more hectic pace as the situation worsened.

That afternoon our house was taken by storm by an army of waiters. In three-quarters of an hour they had set up little tables everywhere on the ground floor, and filled the trough in the kitchen garden with bottles of champagne and crushed ice. About nine o'clock I went with my mother to Vichy, where we witnessed a gala showing of the film *L'Eternel Retour*, and then went on to the Japanese embassy to see an exhibition of Judo. Towards midnight, accompanied by Jean Marais, Madeleine Sologne and a whole crowd of people, we came home to supper, the house having been turned into a grand hotel for one night. Dr. Ménestrel, the Marshal's doctor, had a little red squirrel perched on his shoulder; early next morning I killed it by mistake, through letting it eat a cherry-stone, a kernel containing prussic acid.

The lawyer Jacques Fourcade, who was later to become President of the Union Française, was quite uncontrollable. He was an enormous fattish man, who spoke with the harsh accent of his native village, Vic-de-Bigorre. He quoted Ronsard, and expressed his contempt for present company by a loud fart. Being unused to that sort of noise I stared at him in surprise. Then he drew me to him:

'It doesn't matter, I'm on the other side.'

That was how I learned that Monsieur Jacques Fourcade was anti-Vichy.

Coco Chanel was wearing the androgynous schoolgirl suit that she had worn for twenty years and that she has even forced a certain number of Frenchwomen to wear up to the present day. She showed an interest in me which was touching, but which had something permanently aggressive about it. That evening, with Misia Sert by her side, she let me have it straight:

'My dear Pascal, you know nothing, you'll never be able to do anything, you're a born goodfornothing. Consequently you'll have to learn to be a pimp.'

Not knowing the meaning of this term, I asked her to explain, which she did. I refused angrily; she insisted spitefully, suggesting that I should begin right away at her expense.

'Old plucked chicken.'

Why did I say that? Perhaps because I had been swigging what was left in a number of glasses. Looking like an Indian on the war-path, she briefly twiddled her fabulous pearl necklace which must have cost the lives of five hundred thousand oysters and five hundred divers, then she dealt me a slap that set rockets bursting higgledy-piggledy inside my head. She was in fighting form, but so was I. I gave her back a slap that made a horrid sound against her pale Aztec cheek. This shocking act caused an immediate uproar in the drawing-room; I was seized, violently kicked out, picked up like a bundle, flung into bed like a prisoner into his cell, tucked in as tight as though I were in chains, and locked in. Then silence. Oh no, *merde*! I was neither beaten nor downcast. Still at top speed, I jumped out of bed, climbed over the window-sill, got into the garden and went back into the drawing-room . . . No good, too late. They had all forgotten me in under three minutes, the ungrateful lot. War, fear and pleasure had absorbed them again. Life walls up madmen, and I was decidedly still too small to try out the roundness of the world for myself.

*

End of Summer 1943. I was taking a nap with a young calf in the farm cowshed when the farmer's son appeared, carrying a sporting gun. He was a handsome twenty-year-old, a hundred-per-cent resister, who always looked at me as if I belonged to the Gestapo. When he saw me there he gave a queer sort of smile. Knowing, like everyone else, that it was forbidden to possess arms, I advised him to hide his gun. He didn't answer, swayed from one foot to the other and said, preening himself:

'Come along with me, I've got something to show you.'

Delighted that he was showing some interest in me at last, I followed him. We went through the farmyard as far as some old deserted buildings. Here he grabbed me by the collar and flung

117

me into an empty pigsty, then bolted the door. The more I yelled the more he laughed. Finally he advised me to shut up and promised to come back and fetch me when night fell.

'To fetch me for what?'

'When one's got the son one's got the father.'

Uttering this elementary truth, he moved away. Alone in my stinking lair, I began to cry. Then fear replaced despair and I launched into prayer. I must have reached my eighth Our Father when I made out in the semi-darkness a machine for crushing nettles. I climbed on to it, managed to push up some tiles in the roof and got out.

I reached the house exhausted, gasping for breath. Father was not there, nor was Mother. Florence was away. To whom could I complain, who would protect me? My brother couldn't care less whether I was kidnapped or not; as for the maid, who had a meal for ten people to prepare, she just refused to listen to me.

That same evening my kidnapper, wrongly convinced that my parents had informed the police, left his parents' farm for good; he stayed with the Maquis until the Liberation and covered himself with glory.

Illiterate though I was, the demon of play-writing possessed me. I dictated to my mother a one-act play: *The Return of Napoleon*. The plot was as follows: Napoleon gets tired of being dead, and wakes up in the Invalides. He leaves his tomb and goes for a walk alone along the Boulevard Saint-Germain. Here he meets a Prefect on holiday who puts him in the picture about the political situation. They go together to the Deux Magots, where Napoleon visits the lavatory and discovers the telephone.

'What's that, what's that?' he asks with a Corsican accent.

The Prefect having instructed him in the use of this instrument, Napoleon acquires some tokens from the loo-lady, telephones Berlin, London, Moscow and New York, and peace is restored.

The first and last performance of this work took place in our drawing-room, in the presence of the local farm people, of

Monsieur Georges Bonnet, former Minister for Foreign Affairs, and of Gunther Diehl, a young German diplomat who was later to become Minister of Information of the Federal Republic. The part of Napoleon was played by my brother Simon. I was the Prefect. The young maid who sleep-walked was excellent as the loo-lady. The end of the performance was greeted with storms of applause. On the whole, I achieved a great success both as author and as actor. Only Georges Bonnet did not appreciate my work. Tirelessly pursuing his favourite idea, he explained to me that at Munich there had been several telephones and that the conference had none the less resulted in war. I terribly wanted to tell him that he couldn't have been as good at telephoning as my Napoleon. His judicious, considered remarks made me boil with rage. Reason which is nothing more than reason has always seemed to me something completely empty. If that man had said to me: 'You ought to make Napoleon marry the loo-lady', I'd have been delighted. If he'd said anything, however non-sensical, I'd have been in the seventh heaven. But he said nothing nonsensical; he talked like a grown-up who had certainly never been a child. It must be admitted that at that period I was hypersensitive. I had not yet endured a slating from the critics. I had not experienced that icy silence that follows the first showing of a film that's a flop. Hurt and on the verge of tears, I decided to abandon the theatre in favour of literature. Only I possessed no sort of grounding, not even the A.B.C. I plunged in blindly, with plenty of inspiration but no culture.

My first theme was provided me on our return to school in September 1943. The teacher at the Charmeil school, having become anti-Vichyist, had introduced a debate among the boys in the top class, including my brother, by insidiously suggesting as a subject for an essay: 'What is your opinion of the Declaration of the Rights of Man?'

Simon, who is a dreamy, secretive, melancholy fellow, good at maths and as clever with his hands as a Swiss watchmaker, had no opinions about the Declaration of the Rights of Man. Consequently I dictated a piece to him, about which I had brooded long and cloudily: 'The man who thinks he has every sort of right violates the Rights of Man . . . Women have no Rights of Man, nor do dogs, it's a shame . . . One should never sell one's rights to anyone smaller than oneself . . .'

Simon got no marks. The teacher read his essay out loud to put him to shame. All the children in the class laughed at him. Although my brother never flinched, the teacher and my schoolfellows looked at me pointedly. I turned crimson. They had realized that I'd had something to do with Simon's essay. The teacher made me come up to the blackboard. She called the class to witness my ignorance, my pride, my stupidity, and my pretentiousness. Suddenly I felt a warm trickle, I was peeing in front of everybody.

I had never before felt so ridiculous. This sense of panic I was often to experience later. At nineteen, as apprentice in a paper works, I stood gaping like an idiot when a storekeeper asked me to do a division sum. At twenty-four, when I was introduced to André Bernheim, who was to become my literary agent, my hands were so damp with sweat that I could do nothing but nod and mutter a faint *bonjour*. My body has always been an uncertain ally which, far from helping me to disguise my ignorance, emphasizes it almost deliberately. Extreme desire may render me impotent. Strong emotions, as well as too much drink, make me vomit grotesquely; I retch in jerks, as though to bring up my chronic anguish and my very innards. It's no fun for anyone to be involved with me. I can draw strength only from my own weakness.

What has always saved me from myself is my permanent ill-luck. The people I have loved have all begun by rejecting me obstinately, and they have probably been right. At fifteen I didn't know how to do anything. At seventeen, a marked man because I was my father's son and the protégé of a rich and beautiful married woman, I was practically outlawed by the bourgeois society in which I had been brought up. At nineteen I started at the bottom of the ladder as a worker in a paper factory, a perfectly futile itinerant career: three months at Bagnolet to become acquainted with the offset printing process, four months at Bègles to learn how to make Kraft paper, five months at Schweighouse in the Bas-Rhin, close to the women's jail at Haguenau, the inmates of which provided factory hands for my firm, two months at Doullens near Amiens making cardboard boxes, three months at Novillars near Besançon to be initiated into the mysteries of bisulphate pulp . . . What a lot of paper I had made before ever writing on any!

After two years that were like an endless tunnel whose only ventilation was on to a cesspit, chance plus the friendship of a young graduate of the École Normale enabled me to leave the concentration-camp world in which French workers still, too often, live, and to join the head offices of the company in Paris. After the seamy side and all the filth I now saw the gilded surface. The smart building in the Avenue de l'Opéra, the polished brass plates: limited company . . . capital so much . . . I had done with the enormous grindstones crushing paper pulp amidst the hellish clatter of gap-toothed gear wheels; with the worn-out valves that were liable to burst and scald you; with the sight of women six months pregnant standing for eight hours on end, checking the cardboard boxes ejected by a machine at the rate of ninety per minute, and of Arab workers whose hands were eaten away by acids. Here at least I had a place in the sun, that's to say some minor responsibilities, a small corner of a desk in a tiny office next to the lavatories (which were constantly visited by the junior staff) and a reasonable salary, 40,000 old francs a month as against my previous 22,500.

I thought my fortune was made. It was not. Summoned to Head Office, I learned that although the new department initiated by my friend was working marvellously, partly thanks to my efforts, I had one grave defect: I had not studied at the École Polytechnique. Consequently the future that awaited me in the firm was a seriously restricted one.

•

The discovery of the condition of the working class altered my outlook on the world. It reinforced my gloomy view of my own origins and of the moneyed bourgeoisie . . . I had never read Zola. I knew nothing about the Commune or the great battles against the moneyed classes. Fresh from my life with Flora, from Flora's beauty and wealth, I was plunged by poverty into a state of anguish from which I have never really been released. For two years I worked in close contact with those who have been despoiled of the very possibility of dreaming or hoping. Constraint, authority, arbitrary rule and hierarchies quickly kill a man's spirit. Prisoners always want to escape, but those who lived here did not even know that the wall could be climbed, and in any case where could they have gone, what could they have done? From the moment they were born the die was cast for them, they were mere numbers, pieces of machinery. There was no life for them, only a series of repeated gestures. And everyone connived at this, including the victims themselves, in whom had been crushed even the spirit of revolt, that last treasure of those who have nothing and from whom has been taken even that which they have not.

Mao Tse-tung once said to Malraux something which might have come out of the Gospel according to St. Matthew: 'We must learn from the people in order to be able to teach them.' It seems, however, that the very opposite of this has taken place, and that industrialists have only ruled by keeping men in the great gaol of organized ignorance. French capitalism has expanded as did that of Britain during the essentially repressive nineteenth century. Fundamentally, it has not really evolved, and the power of money still retains an element of police authority which holds the seeds of its own destruction.

The months that I spent in the factory of Novillars confirmed my feeling that the life of the proletariat is a ghetto from which one can only emerge feet foremost; that people don't get rich by working there, only old. You're not taking part in any human activity but only with fragments of a whole of whose causes and circumstances you remain ignorant. Very soon the machine makes a machine of you, and you break up before it does, without having understood anything . . .

It was stormy weather for me again. But this time I seized my opportunity. I was determined to eat my two meals a day and to provide my first wife and our daughter with a roof over their heads. I launched out into business on my own, and collaborated enthusiastically with a friend newly back from Gabon who was starting up the first credit-card business in France, Universal Travellers, which has since then been swallowed up by an American giant. Everything was going smoothly when a woman caused trouble between my boss and myself. On my beam-ends once again, I made for Switzerland, where I wrote the libretto for a romantic operetta with music by Claude Trenet, brother of Charles. Armed with records of the eight or ten principal songs in this ridiculous work, I went back to Paris to lay siege to Albert Willemetz at the Bouffes-Parisiens theatre. He eventually agreed to see me, and after a brief audition, dismissed the operetta as execrable. In despair, after a fruitless attempt to become a taxi-driver in Lausanne, I returned to Paris, where I became a journalist. When at last I managed to make my way into films I was twenty-three. The *nouvelle vague* had just made its appearance, but none of its inventors ever recognized me as an ally. I chafed for five years, condemned to writing scripts for the lowest category of films. Furious at the thought that nobody took any interest in what I had to say, I decided once again to manage on my own, without Chabrol or Truffaut or anybody else. My first scenarios, inchoate and inarticulate comments on contemporary sex, were shot by ex-paratroopers from Indo-China, who had come into film by way of newsreels, and a variety of craftsmen more fitted for low farce than for introducing order into my contradictory ambitions. The results were soon seen, and they were startling, to say the least. In the finished films, not only was my work not transposed and reinvented as it is in a real production, but it was so distorted as to be absolutely unacceptable. Such proceedings could not go forever unnoticed. The critics soon spotted me and slated me severely. Even when

I came to collaborate in films which are practically classics, such as Claude Sautet's *Classe tous risques*, the critics ignored me as though redemption was forbidden me. When I signed the scripts of highly successful films such as *Le Tonnerre de Dieu* by Denys de la Patellière, they abused me none the less, and if I happen to put a foot wrong they inevitably trample on me.

Thus, subjected to the strangest sort of financial difficulties and disasters, from my earliest childhood I've been tossed about and beaten down by life; and each time I re-emerge more battered but also with a keener edge. I learned to read at fifteen. Why shouldn't I eventually learn to write at forty?

◆

Autumn 1943. Fag-end hunting is a bit like fishing, you have to get up early or you come back empty-handed. About six in the morning I got dressed and went softly down into the drawing-room. I knew beforehand that the harvest would be a good one. There had been ten people there talking to my father until four in the morning. The air was still warm. Prime Minister Laval had telephoned twice and the Marshal once. On such occasions people smoke like chimneys.

In a few minutes I had recovered from ashtrays and saucers enough to make up at least two packets of cigarettes, which would put me in favour at the farm for a week or more. Bearing my precious booty, I crept slowly up the stairs, careful to avoid any creaking from the jointed wooden soles of my only pair of shoes. I reached the landing. The door of my parents' room was flung open. Father appeared, gun in hand, wild with rage. He said he had been just about to shoot me through the door. Then he hugged me roughly, flung me into my bed and announced that he was going to take me to Paris with him for dinner and that we should both stay at the Hôtel Matignon in the Rue de Varenne.*
Nobody having told me that this 'hotel' had never let rooms to

* Official residence of the French Prime Minister in Paris: equivalent to No. 10 Downing Street.

anyone and that its distinction was solely political, I was quite mistakenly delighted.

We travelled at our usual rate, an average of 150 kilometres per hour, along a completely empty road. After an hour I felt car-sick. I begged Father to stop. He refused, but offered me his hat.

As soon as we reached the residence of the Prime Minister I was handed over to a venerable old fellow in a sort of theatrical costume with a silver chain round his neck. I asked him where the guests stayed. He stared at me idiotically and laughed wheezily, making an odd gurgle through his hollow teeth.

The quarters to which I was confined in charge of this gloomy jailor had walls and ceilings on which were painted angelic figures with animals' faces and long tails. I learned much later that this was the 'monkey room' painted by Lebrun.

The french windows opened on to an immense garden at the far end of which stood a little Temple of Love, which for the time being contained a couple of policemen. After an interminable lapse of time I confessed to the dodderer that I wanted to pee. The old fellow drew himself up:

'Kindly follow me, Monsieur.'

We wound our way through a maze of passages. Eventually he deposited me at the entrance to a gigantic water-closet.

'Will Monsieur be able to find his way back alone?'

I nodded. He left me. I got lost. I wandered about. I explored, and finally found my father in a sumptuous room panelled in white and gold, busily speaking on three telephones at once.

That evening we ate at Lipp's in the Boulevard Saint-Germain. Monsieur Caze, the *patron*, explained to us that we could either eat or drink. Beer or sauerkraut, not both. Finally we got some hot Bovril with Baltic herrings.

My night at Matignon was peculiarly sinister. I could hear a policeman marching up and down below my window. Next morning Jules Antonini, secretary-general of the S.N.C.F. (French Railways), came to have breakfast with us. He was thin and sad. We drank colourless coffee in which we dunked slices of black bread spread with a tar-like jam. As I pointed out to him that his hands were dirty, he confessed that he'd had no soap for three weeks. Then he turned to my father and said, in a tone of distress:

'Dear Jean, what a terrible year.'

On our way home, at Moulins, about nine at night, in a dark town that seemed completely dead, we stopped and drummed at the door of a garage.

An unprepossessing giant emerged at last. When he saw the tricolor cockade on the car he refused to serve us. As there was not enough petrol to take us back to Vichy, my father insisted. The man was clearly moved by deadly hatred, which must have been very deep-rooted—a son killed by the Germans or possibly something even worse. He took a spanner and marched towards us with the obvious intention of killing us. My father quickly pulled out his gun. He held me close to his left leg. I could see in his right hand the barrel of the revolver aimed at the face of the garage owner, who stopped short.

After an interminable silence the giant threw down his spanner and started to serve us. He pumped without a word, his eyes fixed on us. My father had lowered his weapon and was holding my hand. The two cylindrical globes above the petrol pump emptied and filled alternately. I felt it was never going to end.

When Father tried to pay, the man spat on the ground and went off without a word. We got back into the car. It leapt along the empty road. A hundred, a hundred and twenty, a hundred and forty, a hundred and fifty; the speed gave me a wholly false sense of security. My father gave me a little secret smile.

'You see, old man, our number's not up yet.'

We reached Vichy about half-past nine. Instead of going straight to Charmeil we stopped on the way, beside the Allier, at a riverside inn opposite the Boutiron bridge: *À Robinson*. It was a curious tavern kept by one Madame Chopart. At different times of day one met there Vichy ministers, German salmon-fishers or members of the Resistance on the run. We sat down at a round table where my mother and several friends, including

Paul Marion, were waiting for us. The conversation turned on the increasing number of armed attacks being made on collaborators. Paul Marion declared that before any of them got him he'd bring down a few. To emphasize his remarks he pulled a huge revolver out of his belt and put it down beside his plate. All these guns had taken away my appetite, and I was very sleepy. Marion patted my head and said to my mother:

'Simone, if you're killed I'll adopt this one.'

I could barely have been asleep in my poor little bed for three hours when I was woken by shots fired actually inside my room. I sat up in astonishment and saw my father with a gun in each hand, shooting through the window, just like in a Western.

And just like in a Western the attackers answered back. Bullets whizzed past. One of them tore open the ceiling immediately above my head. My eyes and my nose were full of plaster.

My brother Simon crawled up to me in great excitement:

'It's a state of siege this time, pal!'

It was indeed a state of siege. The telephone wires connecting our house directly with the seat of government had been cut. We could not ask for help. In any case, who could we have asked? Nobody could be relied on. And we didn't even know who was attacking us. *Agents provocateurs* of the Gestapo? Thieves, *miliciens*, peasants whose sons had been deported to Germany?

The chauffeur came into my room in his vest, with a sporting gun in each hand: 'Boss, I'm going to attempt a sortie!'

His proposal, as brave as it was idiotic, was nearly drowned by an appalling din. One of our besiegers had thrown a grenade through a trapdoor into the coal cellar. Now the coal cellar was just under Monique's room, Monique being the little maid who suffered from fits and from anorexia nervosa and was Dr. Giraudoux's patient. The explosion was so violent that it blew up part of the bedroom floor and covered the wretched girl in a cloud of coal-dust. This incident, which was really more funny than dramatic, finally tipped over her unsteady reason. She spent the rest of the night in the drawing-room, standing on the billiard table, nearly naked and with arms outstretched, invoking the devil.

A few nights later I was roused from my first sleep not by shots but by cries which had nothing human about them. Howls rang out all round the house, coming nearer and then moving away to a seemingly tireless rhythm, as though in a dance.

The prevalent lunacy was such that, throwing prudence to the winds, all the men in the house went out with their weapons. It was raining and blowing and totally dark. As soon as one got near the areas where the howls came from, the enemy seemed to retreat . . . Only at dawn was it discovered that hundreds of sheep which were kept in the fields round the house had been bled and horribly mutilated. Some of them were still alive, although they had been partially devoured.

An inquiry was set going, and the most disturbing rumours circulated in the village. There was talk of maniacs and even of a pack of wolves. On the following nights there were fresh attacks on flocks of sheep in the neighbourhood. Eventually a group of farmers got hold of two of the criminals; the rest took flight. The culprits were a pack of farm dogs which had organized themselves, in some extraordinary way, into a commando group, and in whom the instinct for hunting and for survival had engendered a vicious cruelty usually found only in man. These famished animals, having been deprived of meat for two years, remained docile companions by day and reverted to savagery when night fell. Grouped around their leader, Pitaine, an Alsatian belonging to our farmer, they worked as a gang under cover of darkness.

Immediately, within a radius of twenty kilometres, all dogs that were not permanently chained up were assumed to be guilty. To preserve such calves and sheep as were still left them, the peasants exterminated their dogs. As they had no more guns they felled them, they hanged them from trees, flung them into ponds with great stones round their necks or even cut their throats, cooked and ate them.

Misfortune makes men kind. Destitution makes them cruel. All these peasants lived in great poverty. Every family had a son in a German prison or in the maquis. They had been robbed of their harvests, their livestock had been requisitioned. So for a whole week they revenged themselves on their dogs. Not one escaped.

Sky, wind and water were in league against us. Storms succeeded storms, the stables were flooded, hundreds of trees struck by lightning. No one who lived in the region at that period can have forgotten the experience; it was like the beginning of the end of the world, the prelude to an apocalypse. Our farmer, old Guitare, assured me that before the war nature used never to be so crazy.

Although we were in mid-October it was horribly hot. My mother lay stretched out on her bed, watching the downpour through the wide-open french windows. In a dreamy voice she explained to me that my father was looking for a foreign town from which he could secretly be in contact with the Americans, the Germans and the English all at once. When I learned that we must shortly leave for Berne I was in despair. There came a noise like cannon fire mingled with the clash of cymbals; our house had been struck by lightning. My mouth hung open as if jammed. A ball of fire ran all round the room along the radiator pipes, scorching the plinth and the wallpaper. Mother did not flinch. She was never frightened, when I was a child.

Next morning the Allier overflowed its banks and flooded Vichy and the surrounding countryside, carrying everything along with it. To get back to Charmeil my father had to make a fifty-kilometre detour every night in an army truck. Soon the truck itself could no longer get through. The telephone lines were torn down and for a week we were left alone in the house, Simon, Mother and I, with no news of Father, with no news of anybody.

At crack of dawn my brother and I went down to the end of the garden. Here we had to stop, for the road was under water. At this point the Allier had become as swift as a torrent and as broad as the Mississippi. It carried along in its muddy waters all its spoils of war: live cows lowing in terror, hens, ducks, aeroplanes, open wardrobes still full of linen, cars with closed windows that refused to sink. Creatures great and small, dead or still half alive, were swept and torn to pieces against the partly submerged wire fences round the fields. An empty pedal-craft sailed past; I rescued a goat and a pumpkin. Simon salvaged a Louis XV armchair and a suitcase full of saucy underclothes. The only cheerful travellers were a flock of geese.

Men, women and children, avid as wolves, plundered the flotsam, often at the risk of drowning. Near me a peasant was stacking a wheel-barrow with rare books, banknotes, car tyres, a telephone. The covetousness that everyone displayed was boundless and indiscriminate. The river provided everything. And everything thus provided, haphazard and pell-mell, seemed miraculous. If you were away for one moment you might miss a fortune. With my fishing-rod I pulled out a little bathroom mirror. I rubbed away the mud with my sleeve and I saw my own face. It was tired and pale and ugly.

At last the rain stopped falling. The Allier went back into its bed, leaving its banks strewn with shattered plunder and dead animals. One morning about eight o'clock three men in black oilskins came up to the house and asked for my father. Fortunately for him and for us, he had just left. The three men in black were the Gestapo.

From that day onwards I saw my father only very rarely, in his office, which was like a prison guarded on every side, with an armoured door like that of a bunker leading to the Marshal's landing. Mother told me that he sometimes came to Charmeil, but only when I was asleep. He would dash in at three in the morning to dodge the *maquisards* lying in wait for him on the road, and left again before dawn to avoid being kidnapped at home by the Gestapo.

◆

30th October 1943. It was finally decided; we were to leave next day in the car for Switzerland. There were heartbreaking scenes as we said goodbye to the farm people. I wept in the arms of Père Guitare, who declared that we should never meet again. He was right.

130

We shut up this rickety windswept mansion rapidly, as best we could, and hurried away. It was a very ordinary place, and yet unique; and when we left it we deprived it of any sort of life.

If you ever drive along the road from Vichy to Saint-Pourcin, and you see on your left on leaving Charmeil, up on the hillside, a huge grey barn of a place with an enormous roof and more windows than walls, the whole thing half-hidden by great over-grown box hedges, you may care to know that from 26th April 1942 to 31st October 1943 this barn was *le château Jardin*, a crazy battleship, a folly, a place of transit.

If my father had known that three of the four bolts in his steering-wheel had been removed the day before by a garage mechanic in the Rue Vaneau who belonged to the Resistance, he'd surely have taken fright. But since he only discovered the fact at Berne, a fortnight later, he cut all the corners close that day, driving on two wheels rather than on four. For after many hesitations he had finally opted for speed with anonymity as preferable for our safety to the fuss of a police escort.

Father was silent. He used both hands to drive, having one Colt on his knees and two more under the wheel. Although he was now thirty-nine years old and about a thousand nights short of sleep, he still had the touching look of a very young man. This journey to Berne, this diplomatic appointment which I naïvely assumed to mean the end of his troubles, really marked the start of a double life which was even more perilous.

Beside him sat my mother, with our dog on her knees; she seemed as remote as if she were leaving part of herself behind her. Her unspoken sadness, added to her natural gentleness, made her more beautiful than ever.

In the back, on either side of our crazy little maid, were my brother Simon and myself.

Through the back window I saw France rushing away at an incredible speed. Would I ever see my native land again, Evreux, my grandparents? For the time being my only home was the car. In a field I saw a shattered aircraft, like a quartered and dis-

membered bird, jetsam of the terror. I touched Father's shoulder
lightly. He looked at me fondly in the driving-mirror, his eyes
half-shut and a cigarette glued to his lips.

'Feeling sick?'

'No, sad.'

He smiled to me and answered with four lines from a poem
by Aragon which he often used to say to himself as other people
might hum a tune:

> *Puisque vivre n'a pu me saouler de la vie,*
> *Et que l'on n'est pas tué d'une grande douleur,*
> *François, le roi François n'est pas mort à Pavie,*
> *Préparez les couteaux, voici le remouleur.*

(Since living has not surfeited me with life, and since a great
grief cannot kill one, King Francis did not die at Pavia; get your
knives ready, here comes the knife-grinder.)

Was it his tone of voice or the music of the words? I felt my
heart breaking. I had seen too many things, too quickly. They
flooded my head, they blurred my eyes. We drove at top speed
through Lyon, an empty, icy, gloomy town whose streets were
studded with notices in German. What was I going to find
beyond? Another life. Yes, a second life was about to begin for
me in a land where peace reigned and the towns were lit up like
Christmas trees. I was to meet Drieu La Rochelle just before he
killed himself, I was to see Paul Morand again and stay with
Bertrand de Jouvenel, I was to make the acquaintance of Raymond Abellio and become his pupil. At night I was to go skating
secretly on the thick carpets of the Beau Rivage at Ouchy, under
the astonished gaze of spies from every country. I was to become
the confidant of a very old woman who had been lady-in-
waiting to the Queen of Spain, and to propel her up the steep
streets of Lausanne, since she had a weak heart. I was to strike
up an indestructible friendship with a fair-haired young man
with pale blue eyes, Jean Taittinger, now mayor of the city of
Rheims. I was to witness the pomp and ceremony of the French

embassy in Berne, with the official seat reserved for us in church, where I attended Mass wearing an Eton jacket in which I looked as grotesque as a duckling in a cardinal's robes. The end of the war was to bring my father's dismissal, his exile—at first in a gilded cage with a private swimming-pool, then in a shabby porter's lodge; my father's comeback; my first love, my first wife, my second, who was to teach me, finally, that night is one half of day, who was to take me with her into a mythical Cathay where darkness is alive with flaming lights, where gestures re-invent movement and where eternity, sometimes, comes to a full stop.

The road went on spinning down at the devil's own pace. Night began to fall. We reached the Jura and were met with early snow and sharp turns. When we had crawled round one hairpin bend we ran into a group of *maquisards* with their guns ready for action. They were standing up to their waists in a ditch. Father took one hand off the wheel and grabbed a gun. We, in the car, said nothing. We hadn't time. We drove slowly past these armed men. They appeared to hesitate, as though trying to identify us. Then one of them gave my father a sort of military salute. Father returned it. The car leapt forward. I never dis-covered exactly why they let us go past. What I did learn later was that the Germans were having us followed unawares, and that the occupants of the Wehrmacht car which was on our heels, and which fell into the ambush, were all killed.

Here was Pougny-Chancy, the only frontier post in the Geneva region recognized by the German authorities. On the other side, Mother said, there's nothing to be frightened of. But what was there to be frightened of on this side? Death? Children, thank heavens, are not afraid of death.

Epilogue

by Emmanuel Berl

I knew Pascal Jardin while he was still immersed in that child-hood from which, he says, one never escapes.

He has always fascinated me, and he has disconcerted me so often that he can no longer surprise me—by his appearances and disappearances. An angelic little demon, gentle and yet tough, enslaved or freer than anyone else, with his feet not touching the ground and yet thrust firmly into it.

I loved his book from its inception—because it is like himself. It may be good or bad. How is one to tell? In any case, it is not insignificant. That's all that matters, for me. Books are like people, transparent or opaque. You either get inside them or you don't. When you judge them, you're likely to make mistakes not only about them but about yourself.

This one interested me for a number of reasons.

Pascal Jardin was nine years old in 1943. I was forty-eight. I saw many of the things he describes. And I don't recognize them. But would Cézanne have recognized Vollard as painted by Picasso?

Did Pascal Jardin himself see what he tells us, as he tells it? I know only too well that memory is a process of perpetual fermentation in which recollections are transformed as well as preserved.

That's the case with all of us. But particularly with Pascal Jardin: he looks at everything with so much passion that he immediately alters what, for other people, the passage of time alters little by little.

I believe nobody is more truthful, more sincere than he is. Yet I am always astonished when I happen to believe, or can even confirm, what he says.

In his case more than in anyone else's, perception, memory and imagination form a whole, and it would be a pedant's error to dissociate them.

He is the exact opposite of Cocteau, 'a liar who always spoke the truth'. Pascal is always truthful, though he may sometimes tell untruths. I think he would be incapable of lying. It's not his fault if the truth should sometimes turn out to be misleading.

It might be a good thing if M. Jacques Monod had some dealings with Pascal. His ideas about 'objective knowledge' would acquire the elasticity, the reservations which they lack.

No doubt M. Monod would reply that he is a man of science while Pascal Jardin is a man of the cinema, and that laboratory work allows of experimental control. The reproduction of a result proves the correctness of the reasoning that led up to it, and contrasts what succeeds with what fails.

But Pascal Jardin succeeds: the scenario proves the truth of the imaginary world that gave rise to it, the film proves the truth of the scenario it brings to life. Objective knowledge implies only a certain mental attitude on the part of the person seeking it—as, indeed, M. Monod himself insinuates. Pascal Jardin's war, his childhood, his Vichy, his first and his second wives all exist.

His photograph album does not always correspond with mine. But wasn't he, isn't he still in a better position than myself for taking his pictures? He is less certain than M. Monod of what he saw, of what he remembers, of what he says. But does this mistrustfulness diminish the credibility of his observations?

Pascal Jardin's brain comprises a certain set of co-ordinates. It sometimes happens that the figures he describes surprise me, when I refer back to my own memory. But have not physical facts always surprised the layman, who is convinced that the sun revolves round the earth and that the speed of light cannot be constant, since bodies can move either in the same direction as light or in the opposite direction to it?

I shall surely not be the only person to whom Pascal Jardin's book will restore a due sense of humility. It does so immediately by obliging us to consider the child's-eye view of the war, too much ignored by historians, those incurable adults.

It will do them all good to think about the scene in which the child Pascal tries to understand what is so odd about the simultaneous presence in his father's drawing-room of Krug von Nidda, paying a call, and Robert Aron, on the run.

They might also remember the passage in *Les Dieux ont Soif* where Anatole France shows Parisians on the 9th of *Thermidor* unaware that anything has happened.

Psychiatrists, too, may learn something from Pascal Jardin's account of his feelings about boots: the innocence of such fetishism, the wrong-headedness of those who misinterpret it and the uncharitableness with which they repress it. I am sorry I cannot show this passage to Jean Paulhan . . . in my opinion it sheds more light on May 1968 than does the Eros of Herbert Marcuse.